A Women's History of Sex

Harriett Gilbert is the author of six novels, *I Know Where I've Been* (1972), *Hotels with Empty Rooms* (1973), *An Offence Against the Persons* (1974), *Tide Race* (1977), *Running Away* (1979), and *The Riding Mistress* (1983). She is the books and arts editor of the *New Statesman*.

Christine Roche's cartoons and illustrations have appeared in many publications, including *New Society* and the *New Statesman*. She is the author of *I'm Not a Feminist But . . .* (1985) and is currently making an animated film for Channel 4.

A new illustrated series from Pandora:

PANDORA PRIMERS

Series editor: Adrianne Blue

The **Pandora Primers**, an integration of words and pictures, is an exciting series of popular books on difficult themes. Casting a cool, assessing feminist eye, distinguished writers and illustrators unveil subjects as diverse as Cinema and Sappho. This is an important new series of succinct, informative and enjoyable books in which each author demonstrates wit as well as knowledge and each illustrator shows us the point of her pen.

Forthcoming in Spring 1988:
written by Adrianne Blue *Gertrude Gertrude Stein Stein*, illustrated by Jo Nesbitt

And later: **Pandora Primers** on *Romance, Rosa Luxemburg, Cinema* and *Virginia Woolf.*

A Women's History of Sex

Written by Harriett Gilbert
Illustrated by Christine Roche

Pandora Primers
Series editor: Adrianne Blue

London

First published in 1987 by
Pandora Press (Routledge & Kegan Paul Ltd)
11 New Fetter Lane, London EC4P 4EE

Set in Ehrhardt 11 on 13pt
by Columns of Reading
and printed in Great Britain
by T J Press (Padstow) Ltd
Padstow, Cornwall

British Library Cataloguing in Publication Data
ISBN 0-86358-051-3 (c)
*   0-86358-142-0 (p)*

Contents

Contents

To Robin
for the support and the arguments
HSG

A tous ceux qui m'ont fait souffrir
et qui me feront souffrir encore, j'espère
CR

Momentous moments

9th millennium BC Agriculture invented, allowing men to return to the home and exert a greater control over women's sexuality.

2nd millennium BC Male Ancient Hebrews develop the theory that they, alone, make babies – thus further reducing the status of women and making their married monogamy (and premarital virginity) a matter of hysterical concern.

6th century BC Sappho of Lesbos writes lyric poems in praise of love, lust and women.

6th century BC Solon the Athenian lawgiver invents the state-controlled brothel.

538BC (approx.) Ancient Hebrews, returning from captivity in Babylon, decide that only procreative, marital sex can be permitted.

4th century AD Christianity – now opposed to sexual delight for everyone – becomes an official state religion.

5th century AD Perpetual virginity of Mary, mother of god, absorbed into official church dogma.

1174 Eleanor of Aquitaine's *Judgment* spells out the rules of Romantic Love.

14th/15th century Writer Christine de Pizan brings an important new voice to the sexual debate.

1498 Syphilis first observed in Europe.

1558 Elizabeth I accedes to the throne of England, giving to spinsterhood – and virginity – a positive, powerful public image.

17th century	Invention of bidet, in France, promotes the practice of oral sex.
1692	Nineteen 'witches' put to death in Salem, Massachusetts.
18th century	Physicians rediscover the function of the clitoris.
1762	Jean-Jacques Rousseau's *Emile* promotes the idea of the 'natural' woman.
1837	Queen Victoria accedes to the throne, giving to wifehood – and motherhood – the seal of establishment approval.
1870s	Dutch cap becomes an available method of contraception.
1885	Articles in the *Pall Mall Gazette* expose Victorian child prostitution.
1887	Annie Besant and Charles Bradlaugh charged with obscenity for attempting to publish cheap contraceptive advice.
1897	Havelock Ellis's *Sexual Inversion* helps to create the idea of lesbian 'maleness' and gay 'femininity'.
1900	Sigmund Freud's *Die Traumdeutung* published – igniting a slow-but-sure-burning fuse that will, in the years after the First World War, explode as a sexual revolution.
1914	The First World War snaps the chains of Victorian repressiveness.
1917	Alexandra Kollontai, in Russia, promotes 'free love' as part of the Bolshevik future.
1921	Marie Stopes opens first British birth control clinic.
1928	Radclyffe Hall's novel *The Well of Loneliness* stamps Havelock Ellis's curious ideas about lesbianism on the public mind – but helps, none the less, to give lesbian sex a higher profile.
1947	Dr Helena Wright denounces 'penis-vagina fixation', doubting 'the efficacy of the penis-vagina combination for producing orgasms for a woman'.
1960s	Oral contraception becomes widely available.

1960	Penguin wins the legal right to publish *Lady Chatterley's Lover* (uncut) in Britain.
1963	Betty Friedan's *The Feminine Mystique* sets contemporary feminism rolling.
1966	Virginia E. Johnson and William H. Masters confirm, scientifically, Wright's suspicions about the 'penis-vagina combination'.
1970	Publication of Germaine Greer's *The Female Eunuch*.
1970	Publication of Kate Millett's *Sexual Politics*.
1971	Publication of Shulamith Firestone's *The Dialectic of Sex*.
1980	Publication of Adrienne Rich's *Compulsory Heterosexuality and Lesbian Existence*.

A sigh is still a sigh

Civilisations may rise and fall, empires vanish, revolutions sweep the face of the earth, but sex – or so we're encouraged to believe – just carries along as it always has, its rituals and meanings unchanged 'as time goes by'. But the notion that love and sex have been expressed in the same old ways since the mists of unrecorded time is pretence. This book denies that whole song and dance.

Before Romantic Love got invented – which, as we'll see, was thousands of years after people did – any person who *sighed* at her lover would be assumed to be bored, or loopy. It took the Middle Ages, with their plagues and wars and religious repression, to forge the link between love, sex, suffering and tragedy.

Courtship is strictly a matter of convention. The ways we have sex are, too. A prehistoric woman, for instance, who was simply expected to lie on her back while some bloke thrust in-and-out above her, would probably have thought the bloke mad. And, though women in the Dark Ages frequently had to put up with just that, it wasn't often that they got there by being *wooed*. While women in Ancient Sparta, to take yet another bunch, might well have thought that the sex that mattered wasn't with men at all, but with women.

Lovers behave in different ways depending on the customs of their time, place and background. And the forces that create those customs can be as apparently remote from sex as, for example, the law of the land, religion, technology – even the plumbing. It took the invention of the bidet in seventeenth-century France, for instance, to popularise the custom of kissing one's lover's clitoris or penis. Before that, the plain facts of hygiene eliminated a whole rich area of sexual pleasure and fulfilment.

1

This book isn't an *exhaustive* account of the ways in which women's sex lives have changed from the time of our earliest ancestors. To provide such a thing would take hundreds of years and a book the size of a mountain. It concentrates almost exclusively on the sexual history of Western women – and, even there, has had to skim over many local variations. (For the reader who'd like to go further, however, there's a bibliography on page 217. Many of the books listed there have given this one invaluable material.)

If we think about it in our own lives, our sexual behaviour is radically affected by forces beyond the bedroom (or back seat of the car or wherever). TV and movies can dictate the way that we kiss, move our bodies, close (or open) our eyes. Writers can influence the things that we say, actors and singers the way that we say them.

Our parents, religious teachers, schools and friends will also have given us expectations which will shape not only *what* we do but how we feel about doing it. At one extreme, if we've been informed that it's 'cheap' to kiss a person whom we've only just met, then we'll either refrain from doing it (however strongly we may want to) or go ahead, then feel vulnerable, angry, even resentful of the person we've kissed. At the other extreme, if we've been informed that a 'real woman' has no inhibitions, then we may feel compelled to fuck with a person for whom we've discovered we've no real desire.

The feeling that we had to 'go all the way' with anyone and everyone who asked us was known, in the 1960s, as Sexual Liberation. Feminists have exposed that joke, but even our *genuine* sexual desires have partly been shaped by what magazines, movies and mates have assured us is attractive – whether it's a question of physical looks, age, gender, character or conduct. And then there's the thorny question of love, which seems, if not to be synonymous with sex, at least to be somehow entangled with it . . . .

More prosaically, sexual pleasures can be affected by worries about getting pregnant, concern about our physical appearance, or fears of not 'doing it right'. No one, in other words, starts to have sex without bringing with them an elaborate baggage of hopes, fears, ethical beliefs, expectations and preconceptions.

One purpose of this book is to show how we and our lovers acquire all that baggage – so that, instead of blaming ourselves when we have a less-than-perfect sexual experience, we can understand the forces that shaped it and see how best to counteract them.

Because, if various historical pressures can change how people express their sexuality, it follows that we too can change how it's done – to make it more to our liking.

Why sex at all?

though no one knows precisely when sex first started . . .
there is at least a plausible theory as to *why*.

It wasn't, as you might already have guessed, because of the zing of excitement it adds to the otherwise dreary lives of oysters, elephants, human beings, courgettes. More to the point, it wasn't even because it's the most convenient method of reproducing a species.

A great many plants and several animals reproduce *a*sexually, by cloning: a method with much to recommend it. An amoeba, for instance, avoids the headache of argumentative, rebellious or disappointing children by the simple device of making offspring identical to itself; and, more importantly, doesn't need to hunt around for a suitable mate whenever it wants to make more.

But, since asexual reproduction can only result in more of the same, it prevents a species from adapting itself to any changes in the outside world. Amoebas have only survived till now because they happen to live in places (ponds, the soil, people's bodies) that are fairly cosy and unthreatening.

Species such as the human species, which have needed to adapt to changes of climate, food, geographical surroundings and so on, have been forced to keep on developing. And the way that we've done it has been by splitting ourselves into two different kinds – and insisting that genes from these two kinds mix before a new life can be created. That way, every generation will be slightly different from the one before it, which not only gives us a better chance of coping with changes in the outside world but gives us the opportunity of developing different attributes. Amoebas, restful though their life may be, are highly unlikely to develop thumbs, learn to walk upright or invent penicillin.

Some species have it both ways. The lake-dwelling water flea Daphnia, for instance, spends spring and summer reproducing asexually, its eggs developing into clones without ever having to be fertilised. Come the harsher months, though, when the water flea needs its offspring to develop new gene combinations to survive, it starts producing not only egg-bearing daughters just like itself, but sons whose sex cells will fuse with the daughters' to make new, adaptable varieties of flea.

Greenflies and blackflies operate the same dual system – and, as a matter of passing interest, it might be noted that whatever Jehovah did in the Garden of Eden, with water fleas and aphids it's the female who's basic, prototypical, essential; the male who's created secondarily as 'an help meet'.

But back to where we were.

Creatures who reproduce by sex alone do have one notable problem: how to arrange for the two different kinds of sex cell to come together. Those that live in the water have a slight advantage – oysters, for instance, just shed their eggs and sperm like mad into the sea and hope that benevolent currents and tides will ensure that the two get together – but land-living mammals can't afford to be so lackadaisical.

In the end, among non-human mammals, it's the female who usually sorts things out. Once, or possibly several times a year, her body will tell her that one of her eggs is ripe and ready to be fertilised and she'll drop whatever she happens to be doing and set out to search for a suitable male. Having found one, she'll use all her powers to arouse him to sexual intercourse – then, quite possibly, set out to find yet another male to arouse. At this point she is said to be 'in season', 'on heat' or, more technically, 'in oestrus'.

What's interesting about all this is how it contradicts the popular theory that men are 'naturally' the sexual hunters, the ones to make the sexual running. If by 'natural' people mean the way that non-human animals behave, then *women* are the ones who should naturally instigate sex.

In fact, though, as human beings we're free to make a choice about the matter. To a significantly greater extent than the brains of other animals, ours are composed – over 90 per cent – of a substance called cerebral cortex: a substance which allows us imagination, the power to organise thoughts and to plan, and which liberates us, to a large extent, from having continually to live in the present, just obeying the dictates of our body.

Among a great many other things, this means that women, as distinct from bitches, mares, does and she-elephants, don't actually come on heat. Certainly, our eggs become ripe in just the same way as theirs do (in our case, an egg every month, from puberty through to the menopause) and some of us may even know when it's happening. Roughly half-way between two periods, some of us may become aware of a 'twinge' that means we're ovulating. But it's highly unlikely to make us leap to our feet and switch off the telly, then rush out into the afternoon in search of some virile-looking males.

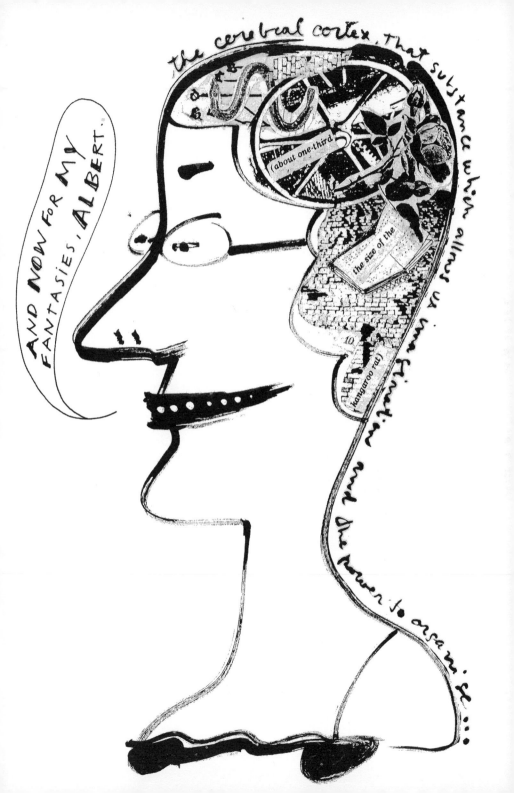

For those of us who haven't the faintest idea when one of our eggs is ripe, this *may*, none the less, be the time when we tend to feel sexiest. On the other hand, there are many among us who are far more likely to be sexually alert just before, during or after a period: the time when our fertility is *lowest*. Either way, unlike in other animals, it doesn't unleash a series of actions that's beyond our power to direct. Our menstrual cycle may affect but doesn't control us.

Besides, a woman can be aroused by all sorts of external stimuli – the sun on her stomach, a passage in a book, a memory of yesterday's kissing – which have nothing whatsoever to do with her menstrual cycle. And often she can be satisfied – usually can best be satisfied – by forms of sex that haven't a hope of fertilising an egg. And a woman can also instigate sex when totally unaroused: through loneliness, insecurity, affection, kindness, a sense of duty – any number of intellectual, emotional or social motives.

Even primates such as apes, their brains consisting of a greater percentage of cerebral cortex than the 'lower mammals', are partly independent of biology, the females sometimes initiating sex other than when they are in season and (apparently) for reasons such as affection or the need for a cuddle.

However it started out, then, sex has become a good deal more than just a means of ensuring that species adapt. Our human brains, in particular, have imbued it with a richness and complexity which *ought* to mean that women's sex lives are fuller, more exciting and interesting than those, let us say, of female oysters.

But, from the moment that women's biology stopped controlling the sexual behaviour of the species, there was always the danger that some other force would attempt to usurp that position: a force not necessarily more concerned with female interests, or female desires, than that which drove them to mate at the ripening of an egg.

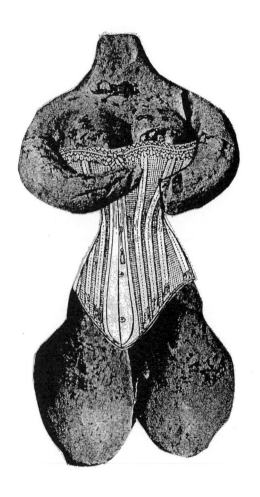

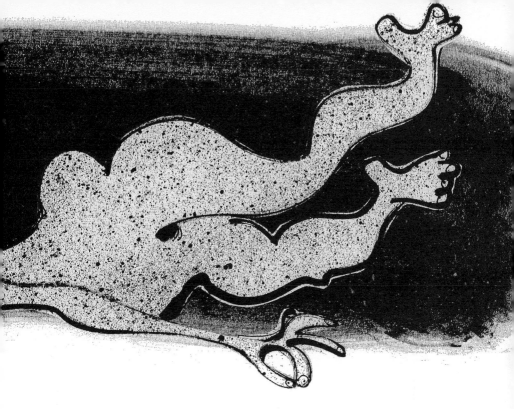

Women as gods and heroes

There's a theory that early, preliterate societies were, in fact, controlled by the females – that it was they who wielded the power and were accorded the status and who therefore, among their other activities, laid down the guidelines for sexual behaviour, decided the premises for sexual beliefs, shaped the structures within which the young were nurtured, nourished and reared.

The first person to argue for this was the nineteenth-century anthropologist Johann Jakob Bachofen. According to him, the earliest human societies were sexually chaotic, a condition against which the women – victims not only of haphazard rape but dangerous, unsupported parenthood – eventually rebelled to impose in its place a system of matriarchal rule. The men were turned into serious, responsible husbands and fathers: protecting and nourishing their families and defending their wives from assault. The power, meanwhile, accrued to the women. It was they who organised tribal existence; it was their homes where husbands lived; it was through them that status, possessions, land and public positions were inherited.

Bachofen's theory was mainly derived from the myths and legends of later, literate people – people who have been able to leave a written record of their lives and beliefs. The Ancient Greeks, for example, believed that the first god of all was a woman called Gaea. She represented the earth itself and existed before time began. Eventually, though, she began to grow lonely and made for herself a son-cum-lover called Uranus, who represented the sky. Between them, they created the rest of existence – natural, human and divine – until Gaea was finally overthrown by the male god Zeus and the Olympians.

The Greeks also told of the Amazons, a nation of independent, warlike women who rode to the borders of their land once a year to have sex with men from the neighbouring tribes. They kept any daughters that resulted for themselves and killed (or, some say, returned to their fathers) any sons.

And almost every other ancient culture has myths and legends centred round powerful women, both human and gods. This, claimed Bachofen, could only mean that women had once ruled the world – since myths and legends are the place where all our collective memory is stored.

The theory that women once ruled the world can either be attractive or depressing, depending on where you choose to focus. What it cannot be is proved either way: we simply don't have the evidence. But, while keeping all options open, it should at least be pointed out that there are flaws in Bachofen's argument.

First, the worship of female gods might have at least as much to do with people's respect for the natural world (for which 'mother' is a common symbol) as with their actual attitude towards living, flesh-and-blood women. Second, such legends as that of the Amazons could as well express archetypal male fears as record a real, matriarchal past. Third, in trying to establish his theory of original sexual chaos (in response to which matriarchal societies were formed), Bachofen asserts that non-human sex lives are random, unstructured, 'promiscuous'. But we know that this frequently isn't the case, especially among 'higher' mammals.

There is another method for guessing how our earliest ancestors lived: the study of primitive societies still in existence. The lives of twentieth-century !Kung, Tchambuli or Saramaka women can't be *assumed* to reflect the lives of our own preliterate ancestors – in Palestine, for instance, or Asia Minor – but there are at least social, technological and economic parallels, from which it isn't an enormous step to deducing parallels in sexual behaviour and belief.

And, if we choose to make that step, we discover both echoes of Bachofen's theory and dissonant, uneasy clashes with it. Most important among the latter is the fact that no known preliterate society is actually *ruled* by its women.

15

Prehistoric sex

* LATER INTERPRETED
BY FREUD. SEE FREND.

Certainly, there is no known society which hasn't both noticed and stressed the phenomenon that one sex possesses a penis, the other a vagina and, when older, a tendency to bleed from that place on a time and scale remarkably similar to the waxing and waning of the moon, the swelling and shrinking of the tides. This particular sex, they would also have noticed, was the only one to get pregnant, and the only one to produce the milk required by the ensuing young.

These observations appear to have had two effects. First, a great deal of effort was made to formalise – indeed emphasise – the difference between male and female. Through ceremonies, rituals, customs and laws – these ingenious human substitutes for the 'animal instinct' by which other creatures are kept from spinning into chaos – our ancestors extended sexual difference to areas of life that had nothing to do with genitals, childbirth or lactation. Women and men (even girls and boys) might be allocated different eating rituals, leisure activities, jobs, costumes, codes of family and communal conduct, patterns of emotional behaviour.

That these extensions were indeed imposed, rather than being the inevitable outcome of genuine physical differences, is evident from their multifarious, often quite contradictory forms. The capacity for strenuous work, for example, can either be thought of as typically male, or female, depending on the culture. The anthropologist Margaret Mead discovered, for instance, that in rural Bali the *women* were generally supposed to be the ones who did all the heavy work. Only when Balinese men began working for Europeans on the docks did their muscles and power become noticeably greater than the women's.

The same is true of the inclination to make-up, elaborate clothes, fine jewellery; or the ability to cook, or weave, or fish, or gather berries. Some societies say that women are naturally better at these than men, others say completely the opposite.

What does seem consistent, however, is this: *whatever a society sees as 'male' it also sees as most admirable.* Or, to put it the other way round, there is no known culture where those who decide what is or isn't important have awarded superior status and value to the daily activities of women – regardless of what, or how vital to survival, those might be. (Just as, today, whatever work is performed by the men in our factories is almost invariably graded higher and better paid than the women's work.) Somewhere along the development of human self-awareness, the male sex took to itself the power to create and define human values, to account for, to direct and to judge the behaviour of both the sexes.

'But how?' is one of those questions with no good answer. Certainly, it isn't due to women's inherent unsuitability for power. One example of a woman who's successfully wielded it – and, of course, there are thousands – is enough to make that hypothesis totally invalid. Which leaves us with women's inferior strength, their menstruation, their pregnancies and, last but not least, the ability they have to make milk. Only these things, originally, distinguished women from men.

The first, women's celebrated physical weakness, has been enormously exaggerated. To a great extent it's been brought about by inferior diet and the social demands of 'femininity': a whole variety of prohibitions on bone-building and muscle development. In those cultures where women are *required* to be strong (as in Margaret Mead's Bali, for instance) they have muscles quite as powerful as the men; while many contemporary women athletes are not only stronger than untrained men, but stronger, or faster, or more hard-hitting than earlier male athletes were.

The limitations imposed on women by menstruation and pregnancy are also slightly artificial – exaggerated, if not created, by a complex of social and religious dictates. Even if a woman in Asia Minor in the 9th millennium BC was as troubled by premenstrual tension and cramps as we are, what was far more instrumental in keeping her housebound once every month, for most of her life, was the almost universal decision that menstrual blood was dangerous, unlucky and dirty. In a similar vein, although she was likely to have worked until she gave birth, the period following birth was probably surrounded by cleanliness taboos.

But these restrictions on women's involvement in public, decision-making life have to have been imposed by men *already empowered to impose them*. And how men acquired that original power must be due, I suggest, to the last female attribute above: the ability and, in earliest times, the obligation to breastfeed. Breastfeeding – with its concomitant tendency to all-round protectiveness and care for the young – would naturally have handicapped women when it came to involvement in decision-making, to leaving the original family group in order to negotiate with other families, to travelling and exploring and coming to conclusions on the nature of the big, wide world.

Whether or not that's how women's subjugation to men's interpretation of the natural and supernatural worlds began, there is little doubt that begin it did, and one result is that women's sexuality became, like everything else about them, an object of male control. In fact, it was extremely important that men and women's sexuality alike be brought under social control. Since sex for humans isn't a simple matter of procreation, but a force involving love, possessiveness, anger and murderous hatred, its regulation is felt to be essential to all societies' survival.

On one level, this can be purely pragmatic – an attempt to limit the jealousies that might destroy a community. On another level, regulating sex can become a kind of appeasement of the gods – so that early hunters, in much the same way as football players and cricketers today, might well have decided that a hunting party would be more efficient and better protected if its members had just had sex. And, if that was what they decided, then pre-hunt sex was what the women would have been compelled to provide. Equally, if the men decided that sexual intercourse debilitates a hunter, then the women, no matter how much they objected, would be forced into pre-hunt celibacy. Individual members of either sex might resent the prohibition or compulsion, but only the men had access to the power-body that created it.

For all that, it's extremely unlikely that early woman led the cut-off existence, centred solely round kids and kitchen, that was later enforced on the wives and daughters of aristocratic Athens – or, more recently, on female, middle-class Victorians. First, however much undervalued, her public labour was needed for society's survival. Second, there would be days, weeks, months, when the men were off hunting or fighting and the women were left in practical control of the community.

Third, to return to where we started, the observation that women alone were capable of giving birth led, to begin with, to a false if understandable assumption: that women alone created the babies they bore. And the repercussions from these assumptions were enormous – especially for women's sex life.

21

Sex for pleasure

If you think about it, it isn't surprising that people didn't at first understand the link between sexual intercourse and having babies. The connection, for one thing, is erratic; one woman has sex twice a day and never gets pregnant at all, while another, as we all know too well, gets pregnant the first time she has it.

And then, the obvious signs of pregnancy often don't occur for several weeks after conception has happened, further estranging the two events in the minds of those who experience them. And, in societies where sexual relations aren't artificially restricted – aren't, for example, forbidden to the young or to couples not formally married – there will be no 'control' group of celibate, childless, post-pubescent women to compare with the sexually active and frequently pregnant ones. It could very well seem in such circumstances that puberty, rather than sexual intercourse, made a woman liable to motherhood.

Even when the connection has been made between sexual intercourse and pregnancy, it still doesn't follow that men will deduce their biological fatherhood, will know that those embryos growing in wombs are partly composed of *themselves*. Indeed, there were recently communities in Melanesia, the Trobriand Islands, Central Australia and parts of Africa, where penetration was seen as an act which opened a woman's body to allow a god, or a spiritual being, to slip along into her womb: in the absence of any knowledge of sperm, ova, cellular fusion or genetics, a not unreasonable belief.

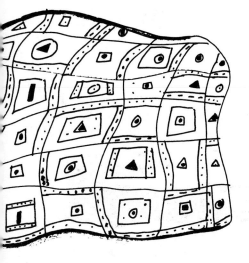

In hunting-and-gathering societies there would, moreover, be no pressing reason for men to start worrying about this. Laying claim to a new human being is considerably less imperative when one doesn't own land, livestock, horses, machinery or complicated houses – personal wealth to be guarded, increased and inherited by one's own. Children, in such a society, can be a pleasure – or a bloody nuisance – but aren't very much of an investment.

So, though early men may have fixed it that *their* desires always came before women's, they had no good reason to wish those women any less sexually active than themselves. That would only become attractive – at least, from the anxious men's point of view – when worries about their children's parentage outstripped their desire for sensual pleasure.

Logic, then, would indicate that early women were allowed to be as keen on sexual pleasure as their menfolk. And evidence endorses the logic. An American anthropologist called Marjorie Shostak, on a 1970s field-stay with the hunting-and-gathering !Kung San people, talked at length to the women of the tribe and discovered that, as girls, they had been allowed to explore their own and other children's bodies (girls' bodies as well as boys') from the moment they first felt inclined – thus freeing them from the ignorance and shame with which more 'modern' girls get entangled.

Continuing to look at what Shostak learnt from the preliterate !Kung San women, we can get quite a full and plausible picture of our own early ancestors' sex lives. Due to their very sparse diet, for example, they wouldn't have begun to menstruate until they were at least 16 – so that a considerable proportion of their sex lives would have had no connection with childbirth. Among their playmates, they would have kissed and stroked and aroused one another with their hands, or enjoyed unforced, unregulated (and issue-less) genital contact.

The first trickle of blood down the thighs would have ended much of that liberty. Potential motherhood meant the requirement to get married. Whether, as Bachofen's theory implies, it's that women need protectors for their children – indeed, for themselves in their vulnerable, breastfeeding periods – or whether because of everyone's desire to impose structural limits on sexual jealousy, violence and

27

possible murderousness, some kind of organised, heterosexual pairing has been common to every known society.

We know that a man who fiercely rejected the role preordained by his gender was, in certain societies – the North American Indians for instance – allowed to adopt a social identity neither strictly 'male' nor

'female'. Religion, the arts, philosophy and medicine offered a niche for those disinclined to be hunters, fighters, fathers, husbands and/or heterosexual lovers. Whether a woman who strongly resisted her gender role – who hated penetrant, heterosexual sex or would rather hunt sabre-toothed tigers than marry – was allowed the same out isn't known. Since societies thrive on the ingenuity with which they accommodate dissidents, however, we can at least say that she *might* have been.

Most probably, though, our prehistoric woman got married – if men were scarce, as a co-wife – performing whatever uxorial task her particular community required, relegated to inferior status less by the power of her husband's fists than by age-old dictates which she, herself, would often have thoroughly absorbed.

WHAT DO YOU MEAN – IT'S ME – WE ONLY DID IT ONCE – AND THAT WAS AGES AGO.

But that sexual freedom she'd enjoyed as a girl, that knowledge of what gave her pleasure and with whom, was hardly likely to vanish into thin air. Though she might be her husband's domestic servant, she wouldn't be *sexually* servile.

If he came too soon, or was clumsy, or brutal, or lacking imagination, not only was she equipped to complain but, if she did so publicly, her peers would perfectly understand and sympathise with her objections. As a present-day preliterate woman, one of the !Kung San, explains: 'A woman may tell about her husband and about how he hasn't satisfied her. She'll tell what she said to him, "What's happening to us? You, my own husband, sleep with me and finish your work. But when you stop and leave me, I haven't finished mine. . . ." Her friend says, "By the time you start to feel pleasure, your husband has finished? Why does he leave you before you feel any real pleasure?" '

This particular speaker, Nisa, is perfectly clear about her own requirements. She objects to men who spill their 'wetness over everything', to those whose penises are too large and to those who have no 'strength in their backs' and so come before she's had time to. She adds, 'When two people make love, the woman moves and the man moves. When they share desire for each other and they both work hard, that's when both become full of pleasure.'

The equally preliterate Trobriand Islanders (studied by an earlier anthropologist, Bronislaw Malinowski) shared Nisa's sentiments exactly. To them the so-called 'missionary' position, where the woman is rendered virtually immobile by the weight of the man on top of her, was a European import as extraordinary as the doctrine of the Holy Trinity.

Our own preliterate ancestors, if anything like their present-day counterparts, would also have been allowed extramarital affairs – so long, that is, as they were fairly discreet and didn't threaten too seriously the peace of the community at large. And divorce, on sexual or other grounds, would also have been quite easy – the main concern of its rules and regulations being for the children of a marriage.

All this may sound too modern to be true – wishful thinking, romanticisation. I can only repeat that in many present-day hunting-and-gathering societies the women *are* as sexually demanding as the menfolk, lovers *are* common to either sex, divorce *is* relatively simple. Repeat, too, that men unconcerned with the provenance of their children would have little motive to turn their wives into ignorant, frightened, unco-operative, passive or disgusted lovers.

If not a bed of roses, then, this was still a sweeter-smelling period than many in women's history. And, before we leave it entirely, it needs to be said that sex for our ancestors was no more exclusively a carnal concern, or even a marital obligation, than it is for women today. Fondness, affection, *love* could also be involved. To quote the loquacious Nisa once more: 'Whenever he went away and I stayed behind, I'd miss him. I'd think:

Gathering clouds

How it happened is anyone's guess. Perhaps our ancestor, blithely unaware of what she was about to unleash, collapsed one day in the middle of a more than usually laborious gathering trip and said to a sister, 'Listen, my love, there's got to be an easier way.'

Whether or not this is quite how it happened, one thing is pretty well certain: it was some time around 9,000 BC, somewhere or other in the Near East, that agriculture was invented.

To begin with, it wasn't so terrible. When the men first started to think about the implications of ownership – of land, of livestock and, eventually (somewhere around 1,800 BC), of horses – they accommodated their desire to protect it, to keep it in the family, to pass it on, within a structure which still permitted the women to be sexually active.

The structure looked something like this: the children born to a man's wife couldn't be incontrovertibly his (either because someone else could have fathered them, or else because the concept of 'fathering' still wasn't fully understood), so inheritance, rather than flowing straight from a man to the son of his wife, must take a kind of right-angled path, via a man's sister, to his nephew.

This 'matrilinear' form of descent didn't do an awful lot for the sister – who was basically a conduit or, at best, a temporary guardian of the property – but it *did* mean that there was still no impetus for men to restrict her sexuality. After all, it made no difference to a man's relation to his sister's son that the brat had been fathered by a heavenly spirit, said sister's husband or the bloke next door. And even if sister and brother themselves mightn't have *both* the same parents, at least they could be reasonably sure of having a mother in common.

But this liberal – if highly iniquitous – system-of-descent didn't last. During the following millenia, men were learning to build themselves cities, were inventing mathematics, astronomy and writing, were devising such ingenious hierarchical structures as kingships: were, in short, growing confident of their power to control 'their' world.

In fact, it wasn't the men alone who were busy building 'civilisation'. The earliest attributable poems still in existence were written by a Sumerian priestess – Enheduanna, King Sargon's daughter – who was born in approximately 2,300 BC. 'You strike everything down in battle,' she wrote to the goddess of love Inanna:

O my lady, on your wings
you hack away the land and charge disguised
as a charging storm,
roar as a roaring storm,
thunder and keep thundering, and snort
with evil winds.
Your feet are filled with restlessness.

But men, by and large, were the ones with the power – and their growing mastery of nature, language, social organisation and so on may well have tempted them to believe that they could more thoroughly 'master' women. Certainly, they were getting themselves in a stronger position to do so.

Those earliest agricultural communities – the women planting and hoeing at their centre, the men often absent on hunting trips or at war against neighbouring peoples – had made a degree of power-sharing between men and women inevitable. But, with the introduction to farming of tools and livestock rearing, the men, as so very often since, came home to oust the women from a place grown steadily more and more profitable. Or else – a move made easier by the conquest of horses as servants – they established permanent, moving homes, dragging the women and children with them, as nomads.

From the second millennium BC, there were horse-and-cattle herding, chariot-driving Aryans sweeping across the lands of India, the Near East, Greece, Italy and Western Europe. And at pretty much the same time another nomadic people, the Hebrews, were entering the land of Canaan.

At which point in our history, we must say goodbye to the tattered remnants of women's sexual independence. Individuals and groups, as we'll see, kept on managing to find ways out – but women's sexuality in general was now, as completely as it ever would be, within the control of men.

The family way

Herding sheep and camels and goats isn't as easy as it looks – but, once you've got the hang of it, it does give you time to think. And during the second millennium BC, as the Ancient Hebrews drove their flocks along the banks of the Euphrates, some of them appear to have come to the following conclusion: since women were undoubtedly inferior to men, then obviously it was the male seed alone from which an infant developed; women simply provided the warmth, protection and nutrition of their wombs.

This was a complete reversal of the earliest theories of parenthood, whereby women alone were the creators of life and men either totally irrelevant to it, or merely its helpers, its enablers. The Hebrews didn't know about women's eggs, so it wasn't any more ridiculous a concept than the old one – but, as concepts tend to do, it soon solidified into 'fact'.

This was for three sound reasons. First, the powerful found the theory attractive: it enhanced their prestige and endorsed their oppression of women. Second, the powerful had a practical need for such a theory: to justify passing property down through their own, as distinct from their sisters', sons. Third the powerful were at last in a position to cope with its most disturbing repercussions: the need to keep women from harbouring seeds from rival males. In short, the theory was convenient to those who were in a position to promote it. And, to more or less ugly effect, promote it is what they did.

When the Hebrews composed the Book of Genesis, their account of the beginnings of the world, there was none of that rubbish about some primal, all-powerful *female* deity. Their god-the-creator was as male as could be and, moreover, his supreme creation wasn't humanity but *man*. Woman, Eve, was an afterthought, something to keep poor old Adam from getting lonely.

In fact, they had quite a problem with Eve. Besides the version of Genesis we know, there were other stories in which Jehovah created not Eve but a woman called Lilith; and, moreover, created her at the moment he created Adam. Lilith, however, was far too demanding. When, for instance, Adam requested that she lie beneath him for sex, she forcibly expressed her indignation: they'd been created as equal, hadn't they? So why should she lie underneath?

For such inconvenient logic, Lilith got herself banished – not only from Eden but from the official Hebrew version of creation. She continued to lurk at their borders, however, a symbol of just how horrid and frightening women could be if not tamed.

In the meantime, second-class Eve – only made from a rib, after all, and a little bit simple when it came to snakes – became the archetypal female. And, although the Old Testament features a handful of extraordinary women – the judge, poet and prophet Deborah; the eventually murdered Queen Jezebel – its backbone is really a long, dreary list of fathers begetting sons.

Their prestige as creators crushed, Hebrew women became more or less like property. In order that they shouldn't tempt men to theft, they were forced, when in public, to cover their face. They were also forbidden, on pain of death or of brutal, physical punishment, to conduct a premarital sex life, to take a lover once married, to divorce an inadequate husband. Their *husbands* could divorce them for any old thing – for being unsatisfactory cooks, for failing to conceive, for failing to bleed on the first occasion they had intercourse – the double standard had by now taken root in every area of life.

After the Jews' return from captivity in Babylon, the rules became even stricter. It became established that sex was *solely* a means of continuing a family line: in other words, only intercourse itself, between husband and wife, was permitted. But it was still the women who defied this, by fornication or adultery, who were liable to get stoned to death for the transgression. And all this was really the fault of those wretched camels and goats and sheep; or, at least – to be fair to the beasts, who certainty couldn't have given a damn about anybody's sexual behaviour – the fault of their owners' desire to ensure that *their* flock of animals passed to *their* sons.

Throughout history, even today, the more that a man's concerned with his property the stricter will be the rules by which he encircles 'his' women's sexuality. While the dispossessed poor have usually condoned both pre- and extramarital sex – for women as well as for men – daughters of the rich have been married off as children to ensure that they were still virgins and, once married, kept locked in the house, the castle, a chastity belt. Even the present Princess of Wales, living in a so-called permissive society, needed to be seen as an untouched virgin before she was allowed to marry her Prince.

To return to those early Hebrew women: some, we must assume, were sexually fulfilled. If, for example, we imagine a woman who happens to fancy, or grows to fancy, the man to whom she's been married, who somehow or other has kept some respect, affection even, for her body, who's fit enough for her wifely duties to leave her the energy for pleasure, who's satisfied by sexual intercourse alone – and isn't put off by the fact that it's likely, time after time, to leave her pregnant – then *there* we have someone capable of enjoying her Hebrew womanhood.

What it was like for the Hebrew woman who found men sexually repulsive, or fancied them, but was left unmoved by straightforward sexual intercourse, or would have enjoyed it, but for the fear of

becoming once again pregnant, or (perhaps worse) knew that every time that her husband rolled over on top of her another round of *failure* to get pregnant was beginning: what it was like for a woman like this, history doesn't relate. Nor, indeed, is it likely to, the chroniclers of the early Hebrew experiences all being men.

Which isn't to say that those men didn't know, whatever their own tribulations, that the women had it even harder. Why else should the Talmud prescribe for a man the following prayer of thanksgiving:

States of desire

Meanwhile, a thousand miles or so to the west of the land of Canaan – a thousand miles from the tents and sheep and camels and fierce, desert patriarchs – another Great Civilisation was stumbling, toddler-like, from obscurity. Through a series of bloody invasions and wars – starting around 2,800 BC when a people armed with metal weapons swept in from our old friend Asia Minor – of diplomatic jostlings, trading agreements, migrations and colonisations, that complex of powerful city-states known as 'Greece' was coming into being: a society still based on agriculture, but also urban, militaristic, nautical and expansionist.

In this society's middle years, there were at least a couple of states where women's sexual emancipation would have staggered the browbeaten Hebrews. One of these, surprisingly perhaps, was Sparta: a militaristic, highly conservative, austere (yes, spartan) state which exerted almost total control over every aspect of its citizens' lives, directing them to the single goal of creating an invincible army.

In Sparta, a girl quite often received an education like that of the boys, encouraged to exercise brain and body instead of systematically having them stunted. As she grew up, she was, of course, required to have plenty of children – how else would the state get its next generation of soldiers? – but it wasn't considered so very important that the children be fathered by her husband. Indeed, if her husband were less than physically splendid, virile and military, it was all the better if she found someone else to get her pregnant. And then, with the men spending so much time either training or actually fighting, a woman was also free to develop her childhood friendships/love affairs with

...WHENEVER i CATCH SIGHT OF YOU, EVEN IF FOR A MOMEN THEN MY VOICE DESERTS ME AND MY TONGUE is STRUCK SILENT, A DELICATE FIRE SUDDENLY RACES UNDERNEATH MY SKIN...

other members of her sex: a desire understood and respected by a culture which valued its women so highly.

It has been argued that societies like this – there haven't been many, but Nazi Germany comes close – are pretty advantageous to a woman. On an abstract level, they must offer her respect as the breeder, nurturer and early trainer of their soldiers. More practically, where children are perceived as belonging first and foremost to the state, there'll be none of that obsession with individual, biological fatherhood – so that a woman's adulteries, her mixing with menfolk in public, her freedom to come and go as she wants will all be supported by law. And, to a certain extent, that's true – but there are severe limitations.

Neither in Nazi Germany nor Sparta were women valued as law-makers, members of government, holders of public office. They were quite unable, in other words, to influence or direct the structure of society. The extent of their role is implied in the words of one of their leaders, Lycurgus, when sneering at the sexual mores of Athens and other of the Greek states: 'For their mares they pick the finest stallions and thereby they produce the best foals – but their women they lock up in houses, watching jealously lest anyone but the husband should father her children, though he might be decrepit, ill or an idiot. . . .' Sparta was run as a stud farm. In it, *some* men might be allowed promotion from stallion to stable manager – assuming, that is, that they hadn't got butchered out in the field as a war horse – but women were uniformly confined to their role as brood mares, as breeders.

A Spartan woman's male lovers were expected to be beautiful and strong (as distinct from imaginative, funny, sexy, intelligent or simply good fun); her female lovers had to take second place to her role as a soldier-producer; and she herself had to be fertile and productive for as long as her body allowed – knowing, all the time, that her sons would be taken, at 7 years old, for the army.

On the island of Lesbos, in the eastern Aegean, women had a different kind of freedom. As in Sparta, they were allowed to mix in public with the menfolk, to receive some kind of education, to live overtly as hetero- and homosexual beings – but this seems to have been far less the result of some organised, Big Brother master plan than an accident of history and geography. Indeed, we don't even know how far women's liberty spread through the social system, since most of what we know about Lesbos concerns a woman from the upper classes: the brilliant Lyric poet Sappho, born in approximately 600 BC.

From Sappho's own works and the writings about them, it appears that both she and other upper-class women were free to live, love and have sex pretty much as they felt like. Sappho, for instance, although probably a mother – her poems refer to 'a beautiful daughter, golden/like a flower my beloved Cleis' – wrote mainly about her desire for, and appreciation of, other women; possibly friends involved, like herself, in the cult of the goddess Aphrodite. Anactoria, Gongyla, Atthis: to these and others she expresses her sensual pleasure, excitement and yearning – and not in any spirit of defiance, but as though such feelings would be quite understood by anyone listening to her poetry.

Later generations have painted Lesbos as some kind of nightclub for all-women orgies – either throwing their hands up in horror or clapping with delight at the thought. (Hence, incidentally, 'lesbian' and 'sapphic' as words to describe female homosexuality.) But, in reality, it seems to have been more ordinary and more relaxed: a culture in which sexuality, both female and male, was perceived as delightful – and not for the soldiers it might reproduce, but simply for its own sake.

As we leave it for murkier climes, the last words should go to Sappho:

> . . . whenever I catch
> sight of you, even if for a moment,
> then my voice deserts me
>
> and my tongue is struck silent, a delicate fire
> suddenly races underneath my skin,
> my eyes see nothing, my ears whistle like
> the whirling of a top
>
> and sweat pours down me and a trembling creeps over
> my whole body. . . .

The perfect housewife

Ancient Athens, which eventually emerged as the strongest of the Greek city-states, is generally perceived as a place of enlightenment, of aesthetic and ethical beauty.

Well, it wasn't much fun for the slaves: the non-Greek 'barbarians' captured in warfare. Nor, to whatever class they belonged, was it much of a paradise for women.

No Athenian woman, for instance, could possibly have written as Sappho did. First, she was very unlikely indeed to have had enough education. Second, the thought of communicating with anyone outside her family would have been as strange as the thought of being allowed to wander the streets. Only were she among the poorest could she go out in public at all: to sell garden produce, or pots, or baskets, to add to the family income – and, even so, she would run the risk of constant abuse and harassment.

Otherwise, the Athenian woman belonged, both before and after marriage, very firmly at home – specifically in the women's quarters – her daily existence centred entirely round housework. No, she wouldn't be starving; and where we now have washing machines, hoovers and electric kettles, she was likely to have a bevy of slaves to assist her; but any woman who is housebound today will know how such a restricted existence can make you want to crouch in a corner and *howl*.

And we, at least, if we want to, can drag the kids to the supermarket, or switch the television on to discover what's happening in the big wide world; or perhaps pop round for a cup of coffee with a neighbour. Behaviour of that type in Ancient Athens would have outraged public opinion – and laid its perpetrator open to the most vicious physical punishment. After all, it was a prosperous state, its economy bolstered by slavery and the wealth from overseas trade – and, as we've seen, the more men own the more fervently they will try to keep their wives secluded. The typical, male, Athenian citizen kept his wife in conditions that have been compared with the prison of a harem.

In fact, they were probably worse. In a harem, whatever else, there's plenty of sympathetic company, plenty of sisterly minds and hearts and plenty of chance, should two people want it, of cuddling, of kissing, of making love. Our poor Athenian could scarcely expect such comfort and pleasure from her husband's aunts or those others of his family with whom she might find herself cloistered. All else aside, the atmosphere was probably crackling with rivalry, with daily jostlings for status and power in the tiny arena where all that energy, all that potential was crammed.

Would the husband, returning from a day of politics, teaching, trade, the gym, rescue our Athenian from her drudgery? Would he chat with her, tell her how he loved her, suggest that they might have sex? No – in the majority of cases, there wouldn't have been even that. Should the husband even deign to return before our Athenian was asleep, he might, briefly, acknowledge her existence, but then would eat his dinner by himself and, having finished, either slip away to the bed of one of his slaves, or return to the city, to his male lover, his friends, a prostitute, anywhere – so long as it wasn't with his wife.

WE SHOULD LOOK UPON THE FEMALE STATE AS BEING, AS IT WERE, A DEFORMITY — THOUGH ONE WHICH OCCURS IN THE ORDINARY COURSE OF NATURE.
ARISTOTLE

Ironically, in 411 BC a play was produced in Athens which juggled with the *opposite* idea. Aristophanes' *The Lysistrata* had the women of all the Greek states refusing sex to their menfolk in an effort to deter them from warfare – a similar tactic to the 'birth strike' suggested by several contemporary feminists. But Aristophanes was prone to wild and fanciful satiric suggestions. Off-stage, the state of affairs in Athens was that, in the interests of the legitimate, citizen-producing birth rate, men were exhorted to *try* to have sex with their wives thrice monthly.

At first glance, there's something to be said for the errant, home-fleeing husband. The mother of his children was, after all, an uninformed, narrow and sexually diffident person, the high point of whose day might have been an argument with her mother-in-law over how best the slaves might sweep the courtyard. But the facts are that it was her *husband* who had forced her into this mould – if only by endorsing the laws concocted by his forefathers – and that, should she try to break out of it, to escape the house or (heaven forbid) exercise her sexuality, he might, with the law's encouragement, kill her. Or (as is still too often the case) cast her out into poverty and social ostracism. He would also, it should be noted, in the case of a divorce, keep the children.

It would be unduly smug to assume that our ancestors didn't have the same kind of guts, the same kind of power to resist as we do. Despite the stiffness of the penalties, some, at least, must have taken lovers, must have sought satisfaction away from their husbands' perfunctory, thrice-monthly thrustings. The ones we know of tend to be those who, as we'll see in the following chapter, survived to become high-class prostitutes – the history of the period was written by the men, after all – but there *must* have been countless others, or those penalties wouldn't have needed to exist.

There must also have been Athenian women who were physically, emotionally and intellectually satisfied by motherhood alone, for whom their husbands' indifference would have been a profound relief. But the fact remains that Athenian men, even more than the (poorer) Hebrews, did all that they could to turn their wives into mutilated semi-people. And, especially among the middle and upper classes of society (those in the best position and with the strongest motive to do so) that, to a greater or lesser extent, has been their attempt ever since.

It does, however, leave them a problem: where, now, to find that pleasure, that stimulation and satisfaction – of mind quite as much as body – that earlier men might have expected, or hoped for, from their wives?

That kind of woman

Organised prostitution was one of men's smartest, most enduring solutions to the problem of having made their wives – in theory, at least – quite sexless. This formal system of commercialised sex was invented, in the sixth century BC, by Solon the Athenian lawgiver – and still, with local variations, with fluctuations in social importance, it forms the other side of the coin to Dutiful Wifehood and Motherhood.

Solon didn't, it need hardly be said, invent prostitution itself. The barter of sex for material goods must almost certainly have sprung into being the moment that any one group of people began to collect more property, wealth, than another. Especially when the disparity between poor and rich became wide enough for individuals to be starving within a generally prosperous community, the temptation – not only for women, but men – to take their sex to the market place must have become irresistible.

No doubt, the idea having taken hold, there were also those who bartered their sex for luxury goods, or for reasons of ambition – the self-same motives that drove not a few of the 'orthodox' traders around them – but the majority, then as now, would have done so simply to pay the landlord, clothe their children, keep alive.

What they would all have had in common, from the weakest to the most manipulative, was the fact that *they* were the traders, their *sexual availability* the goods: a situation at least more hopeful than that of the Athenian slaves. These, whether used as labourers, as house servants or as private whores, were, in themselves, a commodity. And, unsurprisingly, it was they who staffed those original Solon brothels: these first institutions where people (women) were hired out to members of the public (men) specifically as sex objects. The prostitutes were known as the *deikteriades*.

If men's relationship with the slaves who lived and worked in their houses was of an inherently abusive kind, it was still, in the nature of the set-up, one undertaken by people who acknowledged that the other had a past and a future: a reality, in other words, beyond the sexual present. Whether this made things very much better for the slave who wanted to vomit each time that her master crept into her quarters, it did mean that mutual respect and affection could (occasionally) grow through the rubble of perversion and terrified powerlessness. House-slaves were (occasionally) loved, freed, restored to their status as people.

Once in the brothel, all that disappeared. There, the consumer/commodity relationship was strengthened by the payment of the entrance fee, the speed of the visits, the quasi-anonymity of both the parties involved. The *deikteriades'* thoughts, aspirations, even their physical being, mattered only in so far as they contributed to the customers' sexual satisfaction. An individual might well try to 'please' the woman whose body he'd hired – if only because of a sense of pride: a 'good' male lover still, then, being one who could help his partner achieve (an) orgasm(s) – but many couldn't have given a damn about her in any way at all. Well, he'd paid to *have* her, hadn't he? She was his to do with as he liked.

Some, while expressing concern for prostitutes, see them as martyrs to the happiness of wives: fuses for men's more violent, perverse or demanding sexual energies. As St Augustine put it in the fifth century AD:

But quite aside from the fact that men's more violent etc. sexual energies – if, indeed, those aren't the product of mythology – shouldn't be unleashed on *anybody* who isn't pleased to accept them, it isn't true that prostitution is beneficial to a wife.

On the contrary, it teaches men to treat *every* woman as an object: as less than a total human being, as a simply definable commodity. What, in effect, those Athenians had done was to set in motion the concept – with us, despite all the evidence, still – of there being Two Kinds of Women: virtuous, sexless, vulnerable wives and tough, sexy, sin-ridden whores. It would take the Christian church to tune this concept to its highest pitch – to present us with Mary the Virgin, on the one hand, and Mary Magdalene the whore, on the other, as women's only possible examples – but Athens had set the strings humming.

Solon the lawgiver's brothels did have some rather more practical functions: first, they distracted the sailors and traders with which the city was swarming from the (albeit invisible) delights of the citizen mothers and wives; second, possibly more acutely, they provided the state, through a system of taxation, with money to finance the military.

And prostitution – however shrilly the establishment may scream at its practitioners – has ever since provided not only the state but the church with an income. The Dean and Chapter of St Paul's Cathedral rented properties to prostitutes in 1287; in 1321, a special agent was sent by Pope Clement V to England to buy a brothel for the church; the Archbishop of Mainz earned money from brothels until 1457; and the Leonhard monastery owned a brothel adjacent to the Mainz gate. The Bishop of Winchester profited from brothels in Southwark, London, until he was finally forced to sell them in 1649.

But let's get back to that Athenian husband as he scurries away to escape the virtuous, sexless, vulnerable wife he's created – if only within his own mind. It isn't *only* sex towards which he's escaping. If he goes to visit his male lover – male homosexuality was both accepted and widely practised as an adjunct to marital, citizen-creating sexuality – it is as likely to be for his talk, his educated mind, as for his body.

For much the same reason, he might, instead, visit one of the *hetaerae*: prostitutes, yes, but not powerless slaves like the *deikteriades* – not even, as were the *auletrides* (another class of Athenian prostitute),

mere entertainers, flute players, dancers. The *hetaerae* were a small, exclusive group of women, educated in art and philosophy and free to manage their not inconsiderable incomes on their own account. They were also permitted to go out walking in public, attend the theatre and involve themselves in the social, intellectual, artistic and political life of the city.

Aspasia (470?-410 BC), the most famous of these decidedly anomalous women, was not only the mistress of one of the leading Athenian statesmen, Pericles, but had a son by him, to whom he gave his name, and lived with him from the time he divorced till his death. She lectured on philosophy, rhetoric, religion, the social position of women. She ran a school for would-be *hetaerae*. The philosopher Socrates visited.

It would be absurd to deduce from the life of Aspasia or the other *hetaerae* that Athenian womanhood wasn't so bad after all. These were, for a start, quite exceptional people, supremely talented, charming, intelligent, beautiful, cunning and sexually practised: the privileges that they'd managed to acquire were undreamable for other women.

Besides, to do as they had done, to step from the circle of a father's or a husband's protection – many of them came from citizen families – was as dangerous as treading a high wire: on either side of possible success lay the brothels, the gutter, the end.

And did the men who had dug these pits, for women who dared to be extraordinary, declare, whenever one of them fell: 'Well, of course, she was asking for it. *That* kind of woman deserves what she gets?' What's the betting? But worse than that is that their wives might well have agreed: divide-and-rule has always been so effective a system of oppression.

A permissive society

Imperial Rome, AD 54. At the centre of an Empire whose influence stretches from Scotland to Asia Minor sits the 39-year-old Empress Agrippina.

She is speeding the transfer of imperial control to the hands of her young lover Nero: Claudius' heir and her son by an earlier marriage.

Claudius' previous wife, Messalina, the daughter of one of his cousins, had not only been in the habit of killing her sexual rivals and discarded lovers but had finally pushed her adulteries so far as bigamously to marry (in public) a young consul-designate called Silius. Claudius, as became the times, had had the two of them instantly killed – and, for good measure, had also killed off all those who'd been vaguely involved in the affair.

Messalina, Agrippina and Claudius were members of the same unlovely family: descendants of the Emperor Julius Caesar, his sister Octavia and Marcus Antonius. Messalina had married Claudius when she was 14 and he 48 and, from the day of their wedding onwards, seems to have had innumerable, bloody, extramarital affairs. When she tired of a lover called Polybius, Polybius was put to death; when a woman called Poppaea Sabina presumed to steal another of her lovers, Mnester, *both* guilty parties got killed. . . . That fatal, bigamous marriage to Silius – more of a joke than a serious arrangement – was merely the end of a long, desperate string of amusements.

Agrippina, who next married Claudius, had herself been wed at a mere 13 to one Cn. Domitius Ahenobarbus: a person described by the Roman historian Suetonius as 'a man who was in every aspect of his life utterly detestable'. He does, however, appear to have recognised his shortcomings. When Agrippina and he gave birth to Nero (eventually to become the Emperor who fiddled while Rome was aflame) he is said to have replied to his friends' congratulations: 'Any child of Agrippina and myself must be a loathsome object and a public disaster.'

In any case, he died of dropsy in AD 39 and Agrippina spent the following years in political intrigue (even against her brother Caligula when he, for a while, became Emperor), exile on Ponza, a second marriage and, finally, that third marriage to her uncle Claudius, now Emperor in turn. How very unlike, one can't help remarking, the home lives of Athenian upper-class womanhood. What social/cultural cataclysm could have brought such a state of affairs into being? How come that the women of Imperial Rome were so unbridled that nothing

– not incest, not the most flagrant of multiple adulteries – was forbidden them?

The answer, despite the popular myths – of the time as much as of today – is that none of them was even remotely 'unbridled'. Such ones as we've seen were extraordinarily headstrong, others may have champed at the bit, but all, in the end, were harnessed by laws as patriarchal as the Hebrews' and the Greeks'.

Except that, for the Imperial Romans, *patri*archal meant what it said: government not by men in general but by fathers in particular. In the early days of monarchal Rome, a woman might have been married by *confarreatio*: a form of union which gave her totally into her husband's power. But, by the time of the Empire, she was in the control of her *pater familias* from the moment she was born to the moment he died. He could, at a whim, retrieve her from her husband and either marry her to somebody else or keep her at home with himself. Or should he discover, for instance, that she'd taken a lover he didn't much like, he could, with impunity, kill her.

In practice, of course, fathers didn't kill their daughters all that often. Relating to them somewhat differently than husbands, they might, on a whim, allow them freedoms unthinkable in Ancient Athens – freedoms further promoted by the fact that Roman men were away at war for quite extraordinary lengths of time (the Spartans had had their battlefields closer to home) and by the general tone of expediency, of pragmatism (as distinct from ethics), that characterised Roman society.

Women were allowed to get an education (commensurate, of course, with their class), to venture from the house, to attend the Circus – and, if they had mothered three children, or were widows, or unmarried and fatherless, to take control of their private money and spend it however they wanted. None of these freedoms was the equal to those enjoyed by their brothers, of course, but what's even more important to notice is that they specifically excluded the right to participate in the state's decision-making structures: those institutions where it was decided what women would or would not be allowed to get away with. In short, although they were given *permission* to do this, that and the other, that same permission might be withdrawn whenever men found it convenient.

EXIT

LOOK HERE
FÍLIA MEA –
IN MEAM HOUSAM
–AND OUTAM AS WELL–
YOU SAY WHAT
I SAY – AND
YOU DO
WHAT I DO!
AND BY
THE WAY
I DON'T
LIKE
YOUR NEW
HAIRSTYLE
SO –
AVE!

One might then ask how Messalina and Agrippina got away with what they did. Part of the answer is that they – and a handful of their Imperial relatives – were quite extraordinary women: not admirable, like the *hetaerae* of Athens, but breathtakingly unscrupulous, treacherous and scheming.

Despite the sexual nature of much of their conduct they

weren't really looking for erotic pleasure and fulfilment. Messalina's terrible progress from sex to murder to sex was more the compulsive behaviour of a child with masses of money, energy and time and nothing constructive to do with them. Agrippina, more in control, was using sex in the interests of power politics.

Her attitude wasn't uniquely female. There were men all around her scheming, betraying, arranging one another's murder. Her ancestor, the Emperor Julius Caesar, had famously been stabbed to death by a group of conspirators; her brother, the Emperor Caligula, was also murdered; and he in turn, while still in power, had murdered a lover of Agrippina's called Lepidus (suspecting him of a plot to oust him from power) and handed Agrippina, as a present, the urn containing the dead man's ashes. Rome wasn't merely brutal; with its Circuses, lions and gladiators, it was one of the first self-consciously *sadistic* societies.

Men who wanted power obtained it by means both ruthless and devious. But they, at least, had a choice. The difference for a *woman* who wanted power was that she had no alternative to viciousness: no chance, for example, of making her mark with a devastating speech to the Senate, or of sailing away to some far-flung land to conquer, subdue and govern the natives.

The other part of the answer is that neither Messalina nor Agrippina *did* get away with what she did. The first, as we've seen, was put to the sword by Claudius when he'd had enough; the second was sent into exile, then murdered by Nero, the son she'd made Emperor.

Not all the women at the palace took those kinds of risks. Denied power, they settled for influence, for whispering to their husbands at night that perhaps they were making a *little* mistake in banishing poor old Whatshisname or in confiscating the *entirety* of Thingumajig's estate. Octavia (sister of the Emperor Augustus), Antonia (Octavia's daughter-in-law) and Agrippina's mother (the Elder) had been women who'd understood the limits.

As, indeed, were the majority of Roman patricians and plebians: women who, if they did take lovers, did so very discreetly, and who, in pursuance of their children's careers, were unlikely to murder their husbands.

Spouses, in fact, appear to have been rather fonder of each other than in Athens, perhaps because of the slight dilution of the husband's domestic power. Sometimes this reached the level of highest drama:

SOME ROMAN WIVES WERE LOVING BEYOND THE CALL OF DUTY.

More prosaically, the lawyer Caius Plinius Caecilius Secundus – one man, in spite of sounding like an entire firm of solicitors – could write as follows to his spouse:

> Plinius to his Calpurnia, greeting. I suffer unspeakable torments because you are not at my side. . . . I spend the greater part of my nights sitting in front of your portrait and when the hours arrive which I usually pass with you, I visit your apartment – it is an unconscious errand, my feet take me there without my conscious will – and when I arrive at your door and find that you are not there, I slink away sadly, sick at heart like the lover whose mistress denies him admittance.

Evidently 'mistress' was still the symbol for a woman who was loved and desired, but at least in Rome it was plausible to apply the word to a wife.

Just as very few husbands, though, would have thought of being monogamous, there must have been wives who used their outings to the public baths or to the Circuses to find themselves illicit lovers. But these would have been exceptional – if only in belonging to the leisured classes – and, unlike their menfolk, would have had to conduct themselves with care.

So why did contemporary commentators – no less than present-day films, novels and television programmes – depict the women of Imperial Rome as lecherous and insatiable beings always scurrying hither and thither to another lover or an orgy? The women-only religious rites – of Isis, for example, and Bona Dea – were almost certainly just what they said: ceremonies where respectable matrons, helped by some Vestal Virgins, worshipped, sacrificed and prayed to a female god. Yet people preferred (and prefer) to believe the satirical image created of them by Juvenal – who, tongue in cheek, depicted the women as working themselves into a sexual lather, rushing out from the place where they worshipped and howling into the night for men to come and fuck them. 'The buckmouse, conscious of its virility, scuttles away,' he wrote.

Even Messalina and Agrippina were certainly made more outrageous still by political enemies, historians and those who lapped up their words. That story of Claudius' poisoning, for instance, is quite without concrete proof. Agrippina certainly wanted her son to become the Emperor and did indulge in some pretty ruthless scheming towards that ambition, but Claudius' personal eating habits were so notoriously disgusting that he might as easily have killed himself as been poisoned off by his wife. And, while we're at it, there are no real grounds for the theory that Agrippina and Nero were actually having an incestuous affair.

These scare stories – about both specific women and women in general – can best perhaps be understood in the light of our own 'permissive' society, another era of erratic advances for women in the public and sexual spheres and another era when establishment voices insist that morals have gone to the dogs, that The Family is facing extinction, that unspeakable perversions are sweeping the world and that women, women in particular, have sunk to new depths of depravity. Whenever men let the reins on women slacken by the slightest amount, it induces in all but the calmest, the ones with the most self-confidence, a terror of Where Will All This End of quite hysterical proportions. Their reaction, understandable but sad, is to pull and jerk and flap and jiggle on the bit.

Flesh and the devil

The one good thing about pre-Christian menfolk's attitude to sexual relations is, and this isn't insignificant, that they did understand that sex was *supposed* to be pleasurable – even, where possible, for women.

Yes, wives were either locked up or subjected to terrible, arbitrary punishment if, released, they dared to behave in the same sort of way as their husbands. Yes, slaves and prostitutes were treated as though they were inanimate objects. But still, if a woman could overcome or circumnavigate these obstacles, she could hope to find herself lying with a person who wanted to fill her body with pleasure, who wanted to have the same thing done and who, if either or both were achieved, would be delighted with the outcome – as, no less, would she.

There was no *guilt* involved in arousal, orgasms, post-orgasmic languor; even if those societies that emphasised procreation – and therefore discouraged all but straightforward, penis-in-vagina sexual intercourse – inhibited quite a few of the methods by which such states might be reached.

The Hebrew poem the *Song of Songs*, although supposedly spoken by a woman, was probably written by a man (or men). But, romantic gush though it may be, it does at least imply the author's approval of female, sexual desire:

> I am my lover's and he desires me.
> Come, my darling,
> Let us go out into the fields
> and spend the night in villages.

78

Let us awake early and go to the vineyards
and see if the vine is in blossom,
if the new grape bud is open
and the pomegranates in bloom.

There I will give you my love.
The mandrakes will spray aroma
and over our door will be precious fruit,
new and old,
which I have saved for you, my darling. . . .

More realistically sensual was the Greek woman poet Praxilla, an inhabitant, it need hardly be said, not of Athens but of the Argolid. Living around 450 BC, she appears to have written abundantly, although, as with so many women artists, only snippets of her work remain, mainly quoted disparagingly in criticisms by men. A brief erotic couplet from her will have to suffice to show how open and easy she felt with her lust:

You gaze at me teasingly through the window:
a virgin face – and below – a woman's thighs. . . .

Among the Romans, Sulpicia is the only woman whose poetry has survived. Of her, we know only that she wrote in the first century BC and that, as her verses make perfectly clear, she too enjoyed her sensuality:

At last love has come. I would be more ashamed
to hide it in cloth than leave it naked.
I prayed to the Muse and won. Venus dropped him
in my arms, doing for me what she
had promised. . . .

Even the male Roman Ovid, though arguably a bit mechanical, was acknowledging women's sexual desire when he wrote in his *Ars Amatoria (The Art of Love)*:

80

The great achievement of the Christian church – in so far as sex is concerned – was to turn all that sensual excitement, that giving and getting of physical delight, that joy which can, at its most complete, invade not just body but heart and mind, into something shameful, disgusting, unworthy of human beings.

Even those of us today who believe that we're sexually unrepressed, who (unlike our parents, perhaps) feel free to acknowledge sexual pleasure as a thing *distinct* from love or duty – if not, of course, always separate from them – are usually aware of a certain amount of defiance contained in this attitude, and a certain amount of ambivalence.

Even with our own lover(s) there can arise moments of embarrassment, moments when it isn't easy to express a particular physical desire. Even with friends with whom it's easy to discuss sexuality in *general*, our own peculiarities and fantasies can pose a bit of a problem. And that's what Christianity has done, even to the so-called liberated among us.

Christ himself didn't bring this about. According to what we know from the gospels, he was keen enough on marital fidelity ('therefore a man shall leave his father and his mother, and shall cleave to his wife') but there's no suggestion that this 'cleaving', this state of being 'one flesh', was something he thought that the nicer kind of person should avoid – even if, as is possible, he himself remained a virgin. No, it was someone *else* who started the rot.

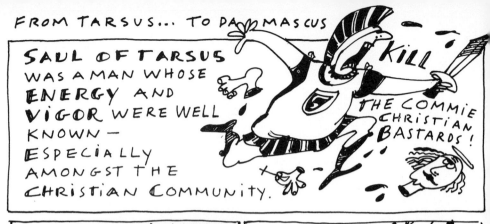

SAUL RECOVERED, AND DURING HIS LONG CONVALESCENCE...

'THE BODY IS AN IMPEDIMENT WHICH BY ITS PRESENCE PREVENTS THE SOUL FROM ATTAINING TO...

...READ THE CLASSICS—.

...TRUTH AND CLEAR THINKING.

Plato.

IT CAME TO HIM IN A FLASH!

SHE WHO LIVES BY THE SWORD WILL DIE BY THE WORD!

WOMEN ARE THE PITS.

SAUL BECAME PAUL — INFILTRATED CHRISTIANITY AND PERVERTED IT.

! ? !

THE FLESH LUSTS AGAINST THE SPIRIT... AND THE SPIRIT AGAINST THE FLESH... AND THESE THINGS ARE CONTRARY TO ONE ANOTHER...

THOSE IDIOTS WON'T REMEMBER THIS...

SO—WITH A VENGEANCE— HE SCRAWLED HIS MESSAGE TO THE WORLD...

ROMANS

PHILIPPIANS

EPHESIANS

CORINTHIANS

...THUS FUCKING UP GENERATIONS OF MEN AND WOMEN FOR CENTURIES AND CENTURIES...

AMEN.

Chastity, though not always achievable, was therefore the highest sexual state. Second, if *unavoidable*, came married sexuality. While sex outside marriage – including, of course, homosexual and lesbian sex – was utterly beyond the pale.

Paul, it has been argued, was specifically teaching for a time of spiritual emergency, a time when the Roman Empire was decaying and the end of the world anticipated daily. But his radical departure from Jesus's Hebrew concept – that sex was a god-given attribute, albeit one specifically to be used for procreation – was possibly also the result of his exposure to the writings of the Greek philosophers. For Plato, in particular, the body was 'an impediment which by its presence prevents the soul from attaining to truth and clear thinking', and Paul may well have grafted this attitude on to Christ's earlier teachings.

Also, obviously, what Paul taught must have struck a chord in his followers – otherwise, the religion would have died along with all the others that erupted at the time. And, though we today might wonder why anyone could possibly have found it attractive, it has to be remembered that many early Christians were slaves (of both sexes) and freeborn women.

These people's decision to reject the flesh, dangerous though it would turn out to be, wasn't altogether absurd: in fact, it can be seen as a logical reaction to the sexual confusion and double standards to which they'd been subjected by the Ancient world. There, sex might have been A Good Thing in general, but freeborn women had all too often been excluded from it or punished for it, while slaves had usally been dragged in on horrible, powerless, humiliating terms.

Probably, had they had the time, such Christians would have modified Paul's fierce dogma. Even now, the Christian churches are shifting their position on a whole lot of issues – the ordination of women, for instance, homosexuality, remarriage in church – and, in the church's earliest days, there were quite a number of second thoughts, revisions, additions, subtractions (even on the issue – rather central, one would think – of whether Christ actually *was* god or was only *similar to* god). But, in the early fourth century AD, the Emperor Constantine adopted Christianity and changed its status from that of a small and frequently persecuted sect to that of an official state religion. Paul's pleas that his followers keep themselves chaste – or, as a last resort, marry – became a legally enforceable command throughout the Byzantine Empire.

And, as Goths and Vandals and Co. assaulted the Byzantine Empire, as Christian proselytisers sped their way through the war-torn countries of Europe – converting rulers who, in turn, more forcibly converted their subjects – the way was made ready for the mediaeval witch hunts, *autos da fé* and Inquisitions.

The Dark Ages

No one – woman, man or child – had very great hopes of sexual fulfilment in mediaeval Europe. Only the natural celibate, the person who felt not one single stirring of lust in body or mind, was in with a chance of contentment – and even she or he would have been confronted with the problem of a body, of genitalia in particular, pronounced by the authorities to be disgusting and sinful in themselves.

Merely being human was, intrinsically, to be evil: a state of affairs which guaranteed everlasting occupation to the priests – as they punished, pardoned and punished again sins that couldn't help but be repeated – but did less than nothing for the self-esteem of their parishioners.

The secular powers' acceptance of this new religion begins to make sense: its founder's *teachings* might have been dangerously egalitarian and radical but, in practice, it was the most wonderful machine for subduing the populace.

Sex, in particular, became a veritable minefield of prohibitions: so much so that even St Paul might have worried. Not all the offences were capital, but ordinary sexual intercourse, for instance, performed with the man *behind* the woman, was considered a crime to be punished by seven years' penance. Any deviation, in fact, from the 'missionary' position was illegal – as, eventually, was sex on any Sunday, Wednesday or Friday of the week, during the forty days before Easter, during the forty days before Christmas and three days before a communion.

More seriously regarded still were buggery, sex during menstruation, sex before marriage, homosexuality, masturbation, fellatio, etc. – any carnal activity, in short, which couldn't result in legitimate heirs. Some of these led to imprisonment, others to hanging or burning.

And death was also a very real threat for any person – especially a woman – who, by living away from it all and keeping out of the mêlée, might be denounced as a witch. Of all the people killed as witches under the church's authority, 85 per cent were women.

The only channel where sex, of a kind, was free to flow unimpeded was that of the parish confessional. There, so long as they were thoroughly reviled, the minutiae of sexual practice could be – indeed, were fervently encouraged to be – gone over in obsessive detail. It was rather like the obsession with which our current 'moral guardians' pursue the arts and the media for 'smut': for words and acts and attitudes which, if deprived of the stigma of sinfulness, would sink back into the common pond of day-to-day human experience.

Not, you might judge, the healthiest of sexual climates: one, in fact, so totally unpleasant that the wonder isn't that people continued, despite the penalties, to misbehave, but that they didn't curl up in a corner, cover their heads with a blanket and die; or else, in intolerable frustration, turn on those who had made the situation with scythes, sickles and forks.

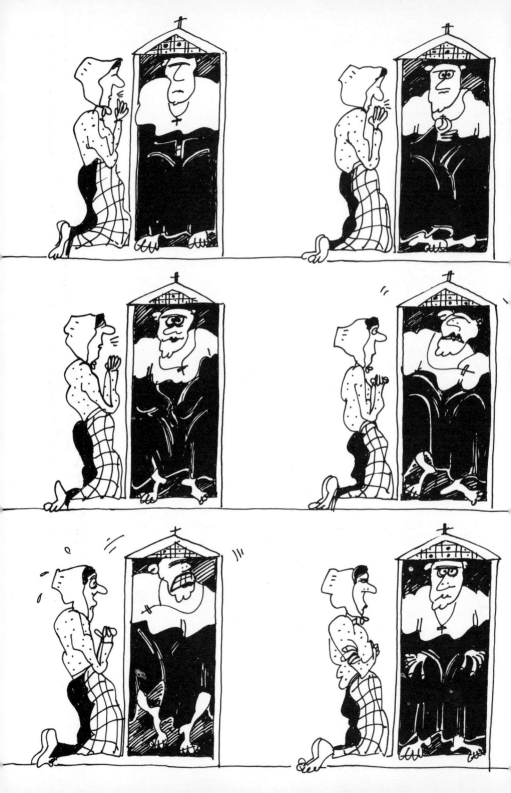

WOMAN
GLITTERING
MUD
STINKING ROSE

SWEET
VENOM — A
WEAPON OF THE
DEVIL-EXPULSION
FROM
PARADISE
MOTHER
OF
GUILT...

FRANCISCAN FRIAR – XIII C.

There are, of course, many practical reasons why they didn't – the need to concentrate their undernourished strength on the business of keeping alive, the lack of communication routes between one village and another, etc. – but, among the less tangible reasons was one provided by the church itself: an ingenious, doctrinal safety valve for *male* frustration and self-hatred. It was, quite brilliantly, simple. Since lust was obviously not about to disappear from the earth – indeed, had it done so, one can't help wondering what would have happened to Christendom – then its persistence must be laid at the door of the weaker, less threatening, less able to retaliate section of the population: the women.

From being equally sexual creatures, who, for reasons of masculine dominance, had to be somewhat restricted, women became *the* repository of lust, *the* door by which the devil and sin kept invading the Garden of Eden. To quote the notorious witch-hunter Sprenger:

> Woman is a wheedling and secret enemy. And that she is more perilous than a snare does not speak of the snare of hunters, but of devils. For men are caught not only through their carnal desires, when they see and hear women: For S. Bernard says: Their face is as a burning wind, and their voice the hissing of serpents: but they also cast wicked spells on countless men and animals . . . To conclude. All witchcraft comes from carnal lust, which is in women insatiable.

If a man got driven to fellatio, or to sex with his wife while she menstruated – or even if his cock gave a tiny twitch as he stretched himself in the morning – it wasn't because he *himself* was unworthy of Christ's great love and self-sacrifice, but because of the evil in women. Even wet dreams could now be blamed on a 'succubus': a female demon who'd assaulted the man while he slept.

None of this helped men feel any better about their own sexuality – nor did it totally free them from the threat of arbitrary punishment and death – but it did, at least, provide them with an outlet for their fears, confusions and angers, encouraging them to treat their womenfolk with morally righteous brutality.

IF YOUR WIFE IS OF A SERVILE DISPOSITION AND HAS A CRUDE AND SHIFTY SPIRIT, SO THAT PLEASANT WORDS HAVE NO EFFECT, SCOLD HER SHARPLY, BULLY AND TERRIFY HER. AND IF THIS STILL DOESN'T WORK, TAKE UP A STICK AND BEAT HER SOUNDLY — NOT IN A RAGE, BUT OUT OF CHARITY AND CONCERN FOR HER SOUL.

RULES OF MARRIAGE XVC.

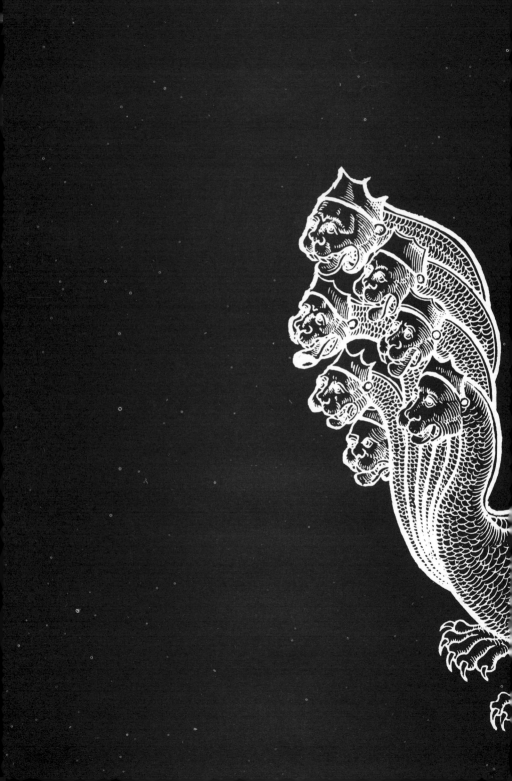

How deliberately the church had done this is impossible, now, to know. Perhaps it wasn't deliberate at all – perhaps it was simply that one group of men, those with the power in their hands, instinctively tended to favour their own when required, by a dangerous situation that they themselves had created, to give a *little* to the powerless.

In any event, the result was not only that women were habitually beaten – doctors, when treating them for other complaints, would note their bruises, their broken ribs, with no hint of moral judgment – but that they were turned into sexual punchbags for men uneasy with sex in general and terrified of women's in particular. Sexual intercourse was fast and furious, no longer a pleasure but a male relief – and a female test of endurance.

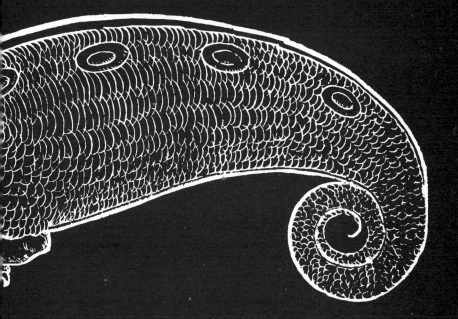

Escape routes

Fetid though the Middle Ages certainly were – in terms of women's sexuality, only the Victorian era can compete – still they weren't totally asphyxiant. For a few lucky women there were narrow chinks through which they might climb to the air.

Before we look at them, however, we need to dismantle a couple of fakes: windows towards which a woman might be tempted but which, if she tried to climb through either, would smash her to pulp like a moth.

Both were constructed from the concept of the Blessed Virgin – as exemplified by Christ's mother. Or, at least, as exemplified by the mediaeval *image* of Christ's mother – for whether or not the actual Mary conceived her first son without intercourse, the fact remains that the earliest Gospel, Mark's, doesn't bother to mention it, nor do any of Paul's epistles; and nowhere at all in the Bible itself is it claimed that Mary *remained* a virgin throughout the rest of her married life and the birth of Jesus's siblings.

By the fifth century, however, Mary's perpetual virginity had become the official church dogma. Historical evidence brushed to one side, the myth of Christ's mother was expanded to include her own Immaculate Conception and, for the sake of consistency, the virgin births of any sisters and brothers that Christ might have had.

Meanwhile, to balance this shimmering mirage of quite unimaginable purity, another 'Mary' was being created from scraps of biblical anecdote: Mary Magdalene, whore, sinner, whose only hope of redemption lay in crouching *behind* the legs of her lord, crying, drying his feet with her hair, then covering those feet with her kisses. Concocted from various women mentioned in the Gospel according to

St Luke, this archetype was presented to women as the only alternative way they could be if they weren't like Mary the Virgin.

Unsurprisingly, many women tried desperately to emulate the mother of Christ – despite the human impossibility of doing any such thing. Still, they persisted and, as I've said, there were two ways in which they attempted it. The first was uncomplainingly to submit to marital abuse, thus attaining the 'purity-through-suffering' that St Augustine attributed to his own mum:

> He [her husband] was unfaithful to her, but her patience was so great that his infidelity never became a cause of quarrelling between them. For she looked to you [God] to show him mercy, hoping that chastity would come with faith. Though he was remarkably kind, he had a hot temper, but my mother knew better than to say or do anything to resist him when he was angry.... Many women, whose faces were disfigured by blows from husbands far sweeter-tempered than her own, used to gossip together and complain of the behaviour of their men-folk. My mother would meet this complaint with another – about the women's tongues.

If this didn't sound like the answer for you, there was always the alternative of sainthood itself – a state which, if you were terribly lucky, led to an actual martyrdom, but was, in any case, guaranteed to develop and nurture masochistic sexuality.

Many mediaevel women, battered both by the church's insistence that they were intrinsically evil and its equal urging that they be impossibly good, not only had masochistic sexual 'visions' but regularly tortured their bodies with elaborate, self-invented penances: binding their waists with tight, spiked belts that secretly ate into their flesh; lying on beds filled with shards of brick; beating themselves; starving themselves.... The Romans may have done us the disservice of linking sensual pleasure with cruelty, but at least they never felt driven to turn this cruelty back on themselves.

There were less horrible escape routes. A woman, for instance, from a wealthy-ish family who turned, as a nun, to *formal* religion – or even one who was pushed to it by her parents – did at least have a chance of pursuing a life of intellectual, emotional, sometimes even sexual fulfilment. The wilder stories of monks and nuns indulging in

THE NUNNERY

BUSINESS PARTNERSHIP

continual orgies, both homo- and heterosexual, were certainly as far from the truth, and probably for much the same reason, as those that winged their way round Imperial Rome – but, at a time when girls were often sent into nunneries as children (boys into monasteries ditto) and rarely for reasons of vocation, cloistral sexuality most certainly existed.

*Hetero*sexuality obviously did – pregnant nuns were not an unknown phenomenon – but it doesn't seem implausible that lesbian affairs often happened too. One, at least, we now know of for sure: that of the Abbess Benedetta Carlini with a younger nun, Bartolomea Crivelli. The seventeenth-century sexual relations between these Italian women have recently been brought to light by historian Judith C. Brown and documented in her book *Immodest Acts*. And even today, when women who take the veil do so more through their own conscious choice, there are many examples of nuns who have loved one another emotionally and sexually. Forty-seven nuns have just told their story in Rosemary Curb and Nancy Manahan's study *Lesbian Nuns*.

But even the nun who lived as chastely as marriage to her Saviour required must often have thought it an improvement on secular marriage. And, since merely by donning the habit a nun had become a 'good' woman, she wasn't *compelled* to go on asserting her virtue by acts of self-punishment.

A second escape route for mediaeval women – though one that only a very few, it has to be said, could attempt – was simply to give up 'being a woman' altogether. Joan of Arc, most famously, just chucked her 'feminine' options aside and assumed the role of a soldier.

Born early on in the fifteenth century, when France was occupied by English forces, this peasant woman maintained that 'voices' had told her to help free her country. Donning armour, she joined the army and, eventually, led the forces that relieved Orleans for Charles VII. Love affairs have been attributed to her but, in all probability, she simply gave up the unequal attempt to be both sexual and a mediaeval woman.

For Joan, of course, it all ended badly. Having secured her king's coronation, she was burnt at the stake (aged approximately 20) in 1431 – declared a heretic, among other things, for refusing to go back to dressing as a woman. A rather happier story is that of Louise Labé –

French, like Joan, though heaven knows if that's anything more than a coincidence – who fought on horseback for Henri II in his expedition against the Spanish and took part in jousts to celebrate that same king's visit to Lyons. Louise eventually married, ran a salon, conducted affairs and wrote a couple of dozen sonnets – of which we'll hear more in a moment.

A more prosaic escape route (and one more of chance than of choice) was that of the woman lucky enough to be married to a merchant or a craftsman – an option which started to open its doors as more and more towns grew up. While such a woman's husband was still alive, her chances of leading a decent life were already better than those of a peasant. She would, to begin with, be out of the rut of total, debilitating poverty and would, moreover, be working *with* her husband at a job that could be both satisfying and prestigious. She wouldn't simply be his assistant, his inferior, but a necessary equal partner. And, perhaps most important of all, both she and he would be far less likely to live their lives in the shadow of a priest. Certainly, the church and its laws would continue to shape their lives, but not with the same intensity as is possible in a village.

Aside from their value in themselves, conditions such as these were likely to have led to gentler, more affectionate marital sex. The point, however, is that even if they didn't the woman married to a craftsman or a merchant had a chance, should she happen to outlive him, of freedoms largely unknown to other women of the period. Even were she the mother of sons, the trade in which she'd become so proficient would almost certainly pass to her, providing her not only with financial independence, but also with worth and power as a possible wife for any man in need of access to a business or a guild-protected craft. She would be in a position to pick and choose, to call the shots, to call the tune, to redress, if only by the slightest amount, the sexual imbalance of the era.

The conclusion – of little comfort to the woman pregnant for the sixth or seventh time, grinding the grain for her family's bread, her stomach rumbling, her vagina aching from her husband's most recent unwanted assault – appears to be that archetypal wifehood, serving and servicing God through your man, is possibly *not*, when times get hard, the best position to be in.

The game of romance

A present-day suburban commuter train slows down as it approaches the station. In one of its carriages, a young woman, to all appearances perfectly fit and encumbered by nothing but a shoulder-bag, stretches towards the handle of the door beside her.

From several seats away from her, there springs an elderly man. Kicking a couple of ankles, knocking the elbow of an innocent spectator, he manages somehow to snatch the handle before the young woman can turn it. 'Allow *me,*' he says with a bow, swinging the door wide open, his merry old eyes a-twinkle with satisfaction.

The woman is startled, embarrassed, confused – she feels obscurely humiliated by having been made to look such a fool, the kind of person who can't leave a train without creating a rumpus. 'Thank you,' she says (for she's not impolite), 'but I really could have managed it myself.'

The man's eyes darken; his lips pinch tight. Humiliated himself, he stumbles back whence he came. 'No wonder,' he says, to whoever might care, 'that there's no *chivalry* left.'

And everyone, the young woman included, has an image of what he's describing: the convention by which, at some unspecific and hazy time in the past, men considered it their bounden duty to open doors, light cigarettes, bear luggage, hold umbrellas, pay restaurant bills for the weaker, less capable sex. And, if treated as a social game, as a little bit of glitter on the bleakness of life, is it such a terrible idea? Mightn't the sense of virtuous achievement that it gives to men who participate be paralleled by a sense, in women, of being appreciated, valued? Where could the harm be in that?

100

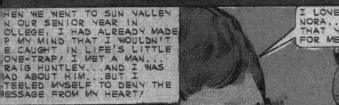

THE LUXURY OF LOVE

HEN WE WENT TO SUN VALLEY
N OUR SENIOR YEAR IN
OLLEGE, I HAD ALREADY MADE
P MY MIND THAT I WOULDN'T
E CAUGHT IN LIFE'S LITTLE
OVE-TRAP! I MET A MAN...
RAIG HUNTLEY...AND I WAS
AD ABOUT HIM...BUT I
TEELED MYSELF TO DENY THE
ESSAGE FROM MY HEART!

I LOVE YOU,
NORA...I KNOW
THAT YOU CARE
FOR ME!

NO, CRAIG...
I LIKE YOU A
LITTLE...AND
THAT'S ALL!

CAN'T HE TELL THAT I LIED
...DOESN'T HE KNOW THAT I
WANT HIM TO TAKE ME IN HIS
ARMS AND KISS ME?

181

1

The original Age of Chivalry – roughly, the twelfth and thirteenth centuries – was bleak enough for any kind of glitter to have been immediately attractive. Militarily, it was occupied by a series of more or less futile attempts to recapture from Muslim occupation the 'Holy Land' of Palestine. Fought for Christ and Christendom, these crusades were no less brutal and corrupting than wars before or since – and, like them, bled the countries involved of human and material resources.

Back at home (whether England, France, Italy, Spain or wherever) the peasants continued to scrape at the land, the burghers to hustle for pennies, the lords and ladies to freeze in their draught-ridden, smoke-ridden manors and castles – and everybody to live with the threat of physical torture or violent death from illness, medical ignorance (this latter maintained by the church's insistence that curing was God's prerogative) and the whims of both ecclesiastical and secular retribution.

Above and beyond these common afflictions, women had extra nutritional problems – then as ever being held to need less of whatever foodstuff was going – were liable to the additional pains and physical dangers of childbirth and were, of course, at the mercy not only of church and state but of individual men.

Against this background, it's scarcely surprising that those with the means, the time and the energy – naturally, the upper classes – invented a second, fantasy world: that of chivalry, of knightly valour, honour, justice and compassion. It's been observed, in recent times, that the harsher a people's actual experience the more romantic will be their art and entertainment; things were no different then.

Besides the stories of the Holy Grail, of knightly adventures and romances, there appeared – in the courts of southern France, early on in the twelfth century – a specific poetry of 'Courtly Love': essentially, of a knight's all-consuming but chaste adoration for a married lady who wouldn't, couldn't, do anything else but reject his impassioned devotion. Those travelling poets the troubadors told this story in their *chansons* and, as it spread into northern France, it gathered around it a complex code of behaviour – becoming a cult in much the same way as Tolkien's novels or 'Dungeons and Dragons' have done in the West today.

One of the most famous courts to promote it was that of Eleanor of Aquitaine (later to marry Henry II of England). She and her followers devoted much time to elaborating on the 'Courtly' rules – notably in the 'Judgment' that they issued in 1174 which declared that love could not 'extend its rights over two married persons [because these] are held by their duty to submit their wills to each other'. In the *Treatise on Love* written twelve years later by Eleanor of Aquitaine's chaplain, it was also proposed that love became *strengthened* by non-consummation, by frustration – that the woman's rejection of her suitor was therefore essential to his satisfaction.

How the Romans, the Greeks, the Hebrews, our preliterate ancestors most of all would have scratched their heads at this rigmarole. Yet, in an age when wars of 'religion' were being conducted via murder and rape and where, rather closer to the home front, the church continued to condone prostitution as necessary to purity – the thirteenth-century theologian Aquinas was only echoing Augustine when he wrote: 'Take away the sewer and you will fill the palace with pollution. . . . Take away prostitutes from the world and you will fill it with sodomy' – tortuous thinking and tortuous feelings were perhaps the most natural condition.

Had it remained a sophisticated game to be played by mediaeval courtiers, it might perhaps have been possible to dismiss Courtly Love as a hypocrisy. Those men, after all, who laid their devotion at the feet of upper-class wives appear to have found nothing startling or vile in the fact that those self-same women's waists were probably clamped in a chastity belt: a ring of metal from which metal extensions curved down and round completely to seal – for as long as the contraption was locked in place – a woman's vagina and clitoris. Nor did it seem to bother them that creatures of intrinsic 'purity' should be thought to *require* such hideous, painful, unhygienic and humiliating treatment – or, indeed, that the women's husbands, away on one or another crusade, were busy violating the wives of Syrians, Palestinians, Egyptians.

But Courtly Love had repercussions beyond its contemporary setting. In literature, it spread out of France to Britain, Italy and Spain, where writers such as Petrarch, Malory, Dante, Cervantes, Marlowe and Shakespeare absorbed its romantic precepts and passed them – strengthened and deepened – to their readers. And those, eventually, started to adjust their experience to fit the conception, to describe their affections and sexual desires in the language of Dante's yearning for Beatrice, of Romeo and Juliet's 'star-cross'd' love, and to shift their expectations of both their own and their loved ones' behaviour.

In some ways, of course, this romantic yearning had to be better than the impotent hatred (of oneself and one's partner) induced by the church. But it still contained innumerable dangers, particularly for the women involved, that are with us even today.

First, it denied women any right to individuality. What they were actually *like* was irrelevant: all that mattered were the virtues that a man had chosen to project on their form. Dante, for instance, only set eyes on Beatrice twice in his life: scarcely sufficient for what you might call a thorough knowledge of her character. He was using her (to be modern about it) as a sex object.

Second, it established the sexual convention by which a woman (however eager) is supposed to pretend some resistance – is supposed to collude in transforming sex into something like stylised rape. It's a tricky game at the best of times (too much resistance, you're a cock-teaser; not enough, you're easy, a slut) and, at its worst, it provides the genuine rapist with his justification.

Third, Romantic Love places so much emphasis on the courtship that the sexual act itself becomes rather devalued. And love-making as an *anti*-climax – besides being somewhat absurd – does tend to result in those quick in-and-outs that do less for a woman than a man.

Fourth, it isn't – was never meant to be – any kind of structure for a long-term relationship. Until the eighteenth century, perhaps, this problem didn't much matter. In life, Romantic Love was mainly the

structure for extramarital affairs, where duration was of secondary importance to intensity. In literature, it was understood that the ending had to be tragic: the climax of Romeo and Juliet's love is their death in a family tomb; Tristram's adulterous love for Isoud, in Malory's romantic *Morte d'Arthur*, ends with him dying of a poisoned arrow and she of a broken heart.

But, from the middle of the 1700s, a spate of novels began to appear in which Romantic Love was the lead-up not only to happiness but to *married* happiness – a clash of concepts so violent that the stories were forced to stop dead at the church. By and large, it was women who wrote these – and almost entirely women who read them – so perhaps they were simply bored to tears with all that illicit passion and death. Marriage (though they must have known very well that it wasn't an eternal orgasm) at least meant social, and usually financial, security. Whatever the reason, such famous novels as Fanny Burney's *Evelina* (1778), Jane Austen's *Pride and Prejudice* (1813) or Charlotte Brontë's *Jane Eyre* (1847) all end defiantly, to quote the last one: 'Reader, I married him.'

And the spate hasn't shown any signs of drying for the last two hundred years. Georgette Heyer, Daphne de Maurier, Barbara Cartland and the untold thousands who write for Harlequin or Mills & Boon: all rely on the implausible conjunction of marriage with romantic love, as do innumerable TV programmes, movies and popular songs, so that our emotional/sexual lives are soaked in illogic and contradiction.

Spreading the word

An historical 'age' doesn't start at midnight, on such and such a day, in such and such a year. What we think of as the 1960s, for instance, had already started by the mid-1950s and lasted well into the 1970s.

As starting dates go, however, the year of 1534, when Parliament proclaimed King Henry VIII 'Supreme Head of the Church of England', is not without claims to being the moment when the church started loosing its grip on the state – and, with that, on the sexual lives of its people. Even in still-Papal Europe, secular values and interests were flexing their muscles.

For English women, the sixteenth century had other things, too, to commend it. The accession to the throne in 1558 of Henry's daughter Elizabeth I need not, of course, have affected their condition for the better (there's no *guarantee* that a female ruler will be of more use to her women subjects than a male one) but what distinguished Elizabeth I from, most notably, Queen Victoria was that she not only stayed unmarried until her death in 1603 but used the condition, deliberately, in her politics at home and abroad: dangling herself as a possible bride in front of the kings of Spain and France, in order to confuse their foreign policies towards her; keeping the men of her own court on edge with her favours and flirtations.

Independence from any one man could therefore be seen as a positive position. Since no less a person than the monarch, Gloriana, was a spinster, to be so was freed from shamefulness or any connotation of repression. The secular, Tudor, Virgin Queen was a very different concept from the Virgin Mother of Christendom – all the more so since Elizabeth's affairs with such courtiers as Leicester and Essex (if not, in actual fact, consummated) were an integral part of the image.

Besides all this, the Queen was magnificently learned. She knew six languages other than English, studied Greek and calligraphy, was a talented musician, dancer, talker, writer and, most of all, politician.

Of course, her accession didn't mean that women all over the country sprang free.

But, in the forty-five years of her reign, women's self-image must have improved – while, on a rather more practical level, social changes were giving *some* of them the chance to project that image on the world.

As the feudal system began to dissolve, the small landed gentry to multiply, the trading classes enormously to increase their influence and vigour, so all of Europe was churned by social possibilities. And one of these lay in middle-class women's access to pens, to paper, to books: the privileges, in the Middle Ages, of nuns and a very few courtiers alone.

Reading and writing may not seem immediately linked to the state of our sex lives. Indeed, in a sexually innocent society – one where women and men accepted their own and each other's bodies as they were, where they'd never considered denying, controlling or codifying their mutual desires – books, plays, poems and songs might have, at the most, a celebratory function. But, as we've seen, such innocence almost certainly never existed. From the moment of our first conceptual thoughts, sex has been *filtered* through concepts – or, in practice, through the use of words: describing what it means, how it ought to be done, how it ought to be experienced and so on. And, in any society much larger than a hamlet or a village, the written word and the printed word – the latter an immeasurably powerful factor after William Caxton, in 1477, established the first English printing press – are far more efficient than the spoken one for spreading a concept about.

Throughout the Middle Ages, for example, we can safely assume that women were uneasy – if not quite clearly and overtly incensed – at the church's interpretation of sex. Those 'disfigured' friends of St Augustine's mum complaining about 'the behaviour of their men-folk' must surely have had quite a bit to say on the sexual double standard in general. As, no doubt, did other women in communities up and down Christendom.

The problem was that they couldn't get together, were unable to pool their experiences and thoughts to start a fair and balanced debate, on the subject of sex, with the men. The sexual theories of the church, however, were speedily, widely and authoritatively spread through the use of written proclamations, or, indeed, through theologians' more leisurely, book-length writings. Of course, there's nothing like having the power to insist – through the use of the stake, or the rope, or the axe, or the rack, or the thumbscrew – that *your* conception is the one that's going to stand. All the same, the ability to disseminate alternative knowledge and opinion is not an asset to be despised by those without, or who'd rather not use, such resources.

And alternative opinions on sex were *indeed* an important component of women's writing from the time, the beginning of the fifteenth century, when pens crept back into their hands. The Italian Christine de Pizan was a law professor's daughter, born in 1365, and widowed at the age of 25. Left with three small children to support, she became an author from necessity, writing a score of poems and prose works on subjects as various as Joan of Arc and the proper conduct of war. But a very substantial part of her output – *The Book of the City of Ladies*, *The Book of the Three Virtues*, *L'Epistre au Dieu d'Amours* (*The Letter to the God of Love*), etc. – was directly concerned with contesting the views that women were evil seducers, that any pride in their physical appearance was a sign of unchaste behaviour, that rape was something they asked for.

'I am troubled and grieved,' says the narrator of *The Book of the City of Ladies*, 'when men argue that many women want to be raped and that it does not bother them at all to be raped by men even when they verbally protest.' The figure of Rectitude, to whom she is speaking, answers: 'Rest assured, dear friend, chaste ladies who live honestly take absolutely no pleasure in being raped. Indeed, rape is the greatest possible sorrow for them.' Rectitude then goes on to remind her of how the Roman heroine, Lucretia, killed herself after having been raped by Tarquin, and how, more positively, the Queen of the Galatians killed and beheaded the man who raped *her*.

By the sixteenth century, women writers were really into their stride – women from the aristocratic, professional, trading and manufacturing classes. The English poet Emilia Lanier, reputed to have been the Dark Lady to whom Shakespeare addressed a number of his sonnets, was the daughter of a court musician. Her *Salve Deus Rex Judaeorum* (written in 1611) is a wonderfully witty and erudite defence of such biblical and historical 'baddies' as Eve and Cleopatra. 'But surely,' she writes in a poem called 'Eves Apologie':

WOMAN IS MORE CARNAL THAN A MAN THERE WAS A DEFECT IN THE FORMATION OF THE FIRST WOMAN SINCE SHE WAS FORMED FROM A BENT RIB — AND SINCE THROUGH THIS DEFECT SHE IS AN IMPERFECT ANIMAL — SHE ALWAYS DECEIVES.
— DOMINICAN INQUISITOR XV c.

BIBLE
ARISTOTLE
PLATO
SAINT PAUL
XENOPH

I AM TROUBLED AND GRIEVED WHEN MEN ARGUE THAT MANY WOMEN WANT TO BE RAPED AND THAT IT DOES NOT BOTHER THEM AT ALL TO BE RAPED BY MEN EVEN WHEN THEY VERBALLY PROTEST..

CHRISTINE DE PISAN
XIV C.

LOUISE LABÉ

PISAN

SAPPHO

KATHERINE PHILIPS

APHRA BEHN

But surely *Adam* can not be excusde,
Her fault though great, yet hee was most too blame;
What Weaknesse offered, Strength might have refusde,
Being Lord of all, the greater was his shame:
Although the Serpents craft had her abusde,
Gods holy word ought all his actions frame,
    For he was Lord and King of all the earth,
    Before poore *Eve* had either life or breath.

The French poet Louise Labé (she who fought in Henri II's army) was the wife of a ropemaker, the lover of the poet Olivier de Magny and was an exceptional love sonneteer – a writer, again, who challenged the male monopoly on sexual assumptions:

What good is it to me if long ago
you eloquently praised my golden hair,
compared my eyes and beauty to the flare
of two suns where, you say, love bent the bow,
sending the darts that needled you with grief?
Where are your tears that faded in the ground?
Your death? by which your constant love is bound
in oaths and honor now beyond belief?
Your brutal goal was to make *me* a slave
beneath the role of being served by you.
Pardon me, friend, and for once hear me through:
I am outraged with anger and I rave.
Yet I am sure, wherever you have gone,
your martyrdom is hard as my black dawn.

Or listen to another English woman of letters, translator and poet Katherine Philips (1631-1664), who's just as outraged by Romantic Love:

Hence Cupid! with your cheating toys,
Your real griefs, and painted joys,
Your pleasure which itself destroys.
Lovers like men in fevers burn and rave,
And only what will injure them do crave.

116

Her words – and those of the other women who were, at last, in increasing numbers, able to communicate views, perceptions and experiences intrinsically other than men's – would have reached but a small percentage of contemporary society. The majority, still, of both the sexes, was quite unable to read. Even the views of Aphra Behn – whose witty, polemical, feminist plays outraged and delighted theatre-goers, by challenging not only male assumptions about the relations between the sexes but also their views on women's ability to think, to write and to create – would not have extended far beyond literate Londoners.

For all of this, the Sexual Debate was finally out of the confessional, had, in fact, *become* a debate, as distinct from a thundering monologue with valiant, but drowned, interjections.

Ruff and tumble

In the rough and tumble of Renaissance Europe, with its social, cultural, economic, religious and political churnings, only a small minority of women were able to grab at the chances: to use the chaos to snatch for themselves new lifestyles, ideas and forms of expression.

CIAO, PADRONE!

There were many who simply got mangled.

Aside from those queens and aristocrats whose blood bespatters the history books (Mary Queen of Scots, Lady Jane Grey, a couple of wives of Henry VIII) there were other women for whom the new freedoms – of movement, thought, behaviour and speech – were at best ambivalent blessings. The new sexual freedoms in particular, as they washed their way down from the court, were fine for those with the ingenuity, luck, money and social position to take advantage of their benefits – but, for most, were often as dangerous as the old mediaeval repressions.

For men, the lightening of sexual guilt, the tolerance of promiscuity, the de-emphasising of duty and the greater insistence on pleasure were, by and large, unproblematic – but, at a time when contraception was a hotch-potch of ineffectual potions and charms, they were likely to carry a sting in the tail (so to speak) for the women involved. Pregnancy was rarely a joy at the best of times. Pregnancy when the father had fled (to another woman, another town), was physically, socially and economically disastrous.

The expansionism of Renaissance Europe had added another problem – though this time one which, physically speaking, affected the men just as much. 'Problem' is possibly an understatement. What it was that Columbus's crew had imported from its first expedition to America, and generously given to the women of Naples, was syphilis.

First observed in 1498, this hitherto unknown venereal disease spread across Europe like wildfire and, inevitably, just as has happened with herpes and AIDS today, was pronounced by some to be a punishment from God. Whatever his role in its creation, its existence meant that the monogamous wife of a less than monogamous husband (Renaissance or not, the most usual situation) was vulnerable to a 'punishment' she'd done nothing whatsoever to provoke.

None of the above is intended to make the psychological and physical cruelties of mediaeval Europe seem less, but it does, perhaps explain what happened in the middle of the seventeenth century.

Back to the kitchen

Puritanism could hardly be called a 'women's movement'. From the time in the mid-1600s when it started to ferment within the Church of England, demanding a greater simplicity of worship, an end to ecclesiastical corruption and a transference of authority from the priest to an individual's conscience, it was essentially a class movement – an assertion by traders and craftspeople that theirs was now a voice to be heeded.

Politically, it was a small but unmistakable step towards democracy. It had little if any regard for the poor (whose state was seen as a sign of their spiritual worthlessness), but it insisted that those who had managed to work their way up the ladder of prosperity be allowed some say in their lives – be allowed, for instance, directly to communicate with God, instead of having his views transmitted by a priest.

Its emphasis on frugality – on eliminating the 'extravagance' of incense, visual decoration, etc., that was still as much a part of the Church of England as it had been of Rome – was unsurprising in a class that had got where it had through steady application, as distinct from fighting, political intrigue, speculation, the exploitation of lands. And, had the movement come into existence a hundred or so years before, it might have promoted women's interests in a way which, finally, it failed to do – for this was the class, remember, in which, in the Middle Ages, women had had the greatest autonomy, the nearest thing to equality with men.

Unfortunately, the increasing prosperity had had the effect of pushing women away from their husbands' sides, as partners, and back into the less prestigious (if equally demanding) domestic sphere. The strength of independent women in the guilds had simultaneously weakened. As crafts became more profitable, more organised, more formal, male apprentices and qualified workers had pushed, to a large extent successfully, for an end to female competition.

But a middle-class woman did still enjoy more respect than her lower- and upper-class sisters. She was valued as a thrifty house-keeper, as a bosom on which the weary merchant might rest his head at the end of the day, as an educator in moral and financial rectitude to his children. Her husband might be absolute master of the house – in fact, perceived himself more and more as a figure of moral authority as his class grew progressively less enchanted, not only with the church but also with the monarchy – but, so long as she obeyed him, she was an asset to be valued, cared for and protected.

It's perfectly understandable, then, that Puritanism, the movement that embodied these middle-class values and attitudes, was attractive to a great many women. Sober, diligent, responsible men may not always be a barrel of laughs, but at least, as lovers, should they help get you pregnant, they're likely to 'do the decent thing' and, as husbands, will probably refrain from excessive drinking, unprovoked violence, constant infidelity or giving you a dose of the clap. Besides which, like early Christianity, Puritanism offered strictness: an easier state of affairs for the powerless (which women still very much were) than whimsicality, moral vagueness, sudden switches in what is encouraged and what will get you into trouble.

There were *limits* to how straightforward Puritanism was: it managed, for example, simultaneously to hold that the sexes were equal in the eyes of God and that, on earth, the female one was inherently inferior to the male. But, at least, it did do away with the cult of the Blessed Virgin Mary, that cynical sop to women's practical powerlessness.

We need to understand its attractions since Puritanism, in various guises, has appealed to women throughout history – playing an extremely important part in the nineteenth-century feminist movement and not, indeed, altogether absent from parts of the women's movement today. We need to recognise that a sex which has tended to experience liberation as the patsy – as the unmarried mother whom society rejects; as the housebound wife whose husband sleeps around; as the person termed 'frigid' or 'not a real woman' if she says that, thank you, she'd rather not, but 'insatiable', 'a nymphomaniac', should she dare to ask How About It? – is likely to view 'sexual licence' from a different angle than men.

Seventeenth-century Puritanism was not, however, idyllic. As we've seen, the family, and the power of the father within the family, were central to its ideology. One of the Puritan poet Milton's complaints about Roman Catholicism was that it had plucked 'the power and arbitrement of divorce from the master of the family'. Beliefs such as these not only restricted a woman's social autonomy, since her duty was firmly to hearth and home and her husband's material comforts, but ensured that, if she wanted a sex life, it would have to *be* within marriage. And marital sex for the Puritan wife – though probably less of an assault to the system than that of her mediaeval sister – was likely to have been on the less than satisfactory side.

Puritans weren't into *celibacy*. One of their spiritual leaders, the German Martin Luther, actually married a former nun; while another, the Frenchman John Calvin, insisted that sexual intercourse was honourable and holy. They were, however, not quite so convinced about the benefits of sexual *pleasure*. Sex, wrote the seventeenth-century theologian Bishop Taylor, should be 'moderate, so as to consist with health', an attitude certainly reinforced by a nagging worry on the part of men about 'spending' too much unnecessary semen.

123

Within the early Puritan movement, there were more radical, exciting strands. The Quakers, the Diggers and the Ranters, fringe groups in which women members played a fairly important part, were far more open to sexual equality than the more mainstream Puritans. The Ranters, who did most of their preaching among the poorest, the squatters and the vagrants, were especially open in their views, going so far as to question the church's insistence on chastity and monogamy. As one of their teachers roundly declared, 'Till you can lie with all women as one woman, and not judge it sin, you can do nothing but sin.'

By the time, however, of the English Civil War and the execution of Charles I (in 1649), when Puritanism became for a while the establishment English religion, it was the more conservative brand that had triumphed. And, lest its worst offence be thought dreariness, it should be remembered what it did to those women who failed to come up to its standards.

Prostitution, though officially condemned, was still the resort of thousands of women whose poverty had excluded them from the middle-class revolution. And witches – frequently women alone, or women whose sexual lives were thought deviant, or women, the so-called 'scolds' and 'nags', who dared to express controversial opinions – were still being hunted and persecuted.

The last English woman to be hanged as a witch was Alice Molland, in 1684; but, as late as 1712, an English woman was condemned to death for witchcraft – though reprieved after much fierce campaigning. All that Jane Wenham – a wisewoman who lived on her own in Walkern in Hertfordshire – seems to have done to deserve persecution was complain when a farmer *accused* her of witchcraft. Suddenly, stories sprang up against her: stories of her persecuting people with cats – in other words, some cats had been spotted scratching at someone or other's door – , stories of her forcing people by magic to do things they didn't really want to. . . . Brought to trial and convicted, she was only saved by a series of delays and, in the end, a royal pardon.

Things were no better in the newly settled lands of America. The notorious Salem witch hunts of 1692 led to nineteen women being put to death – and it may not be entirely a coincidence that America's classic novel of Puritan smugness, fervour and self-righteousness, Nathaniel Hawthorne's *The Scarlet Letter*, was written by a man not only born in Salem but descended from one of its witch-trial judges.

Hawthorne's novel, though published in 1850, is set in the seventeenth century and sheds a harsh light on that era. It's the story of a woman called Hester Prynne who is convicted of adultery by her fellow citizens and, as a penance, forced to wear the scarlet letter 'A'. Her lover (whose name she refuses to reveal), though inwardly torn with remorse, is, of course, never brought to justice. So much for the freedom and equality of those seventeenth-century pioneer women who were helping to forge the New World.

Hidden currents

While Puritanism drove women, children and men all over America, in England, from 1660 onwards, there was once more a monarch, Charles II, on the throne. But Puritan energy kept on pushing at the structures of state and society, creating a potent counterforce to the hedonistic, morally flexible, cynical, tolerant power of the king. Indeed, all over Europe now, there was a similar pressure of currents from opposing ethical/political positions. Enormous changes were brewing.

It's possible to look at history, especially the history of our sex lives, as though it were nothing but a pendulum swinging from repression to permissiveness and back again. It would, for instance, be easy to see the latter half of the seventeenth century and most of the eighteenth centuries as merely a time of renewed sexual licence, a re-run of the Tudor age, of Imperial Rome, of that preliterate era when property and sex hadn't merged. But every swing takes us somewhere strange, somewhere with new possibilities and dangers, somewhere where all the events, ideas, discoveries, disasters and successes of the past have created an untried concoction.

Certainly, it can't be denied that this *was* an age of sexual licence – the tone being set, with clarity and force, by the monarchs of Europe themselves. They called their renewed enthusiasm for sexual activity 'Gallantry' – defined, by the French philosopher Montesquieu, as 'a light and delicate pretension of love' – and those around them were quick to get the idea. The English actress Nell Gwynne became quite openly Charles II's mistress (so openly, indeed, that the King's Road in London is named from the route between her home and his); as, to name but a couple more, the Duchess of Portsmouth and Hortense Mancini. Louis XIV, the Sun King, had a stream of official mistresses (and a wife, Madame Maintenon, whom he not insignificantly married in far greater secret). Augustus, Elector of Hanover and King of Poland, had 354 acknowledged illegitimate children. In Prussia, Frederick William II invented the post of *maîtresse en titre* (approximately, Regular Mistress).

For a woman to be a 'mistress' today implies all kinds of insecurity. Her affair will probably take second place to her lover's commitment to his children and wife – so that any plans she makes with him are liable to last-minute changes. Often, too, the relationship will be secret – compelling the mistress to wait for *him* to write to her, ring, come and visit. And these days, too, she's very unlikely to be 'kept'. Certainly, there are professionals, but your average mistress is far more likely to be earning her living in an office, a school or a factory – not precisely the glamorous, champagne-in-bed Other Woman of mythology.

Of course, some women believe that this kind of life has its compensations: not, for them, the snoring hulk with his dentures out in front of the telly, the querulous boy wanting clothes to be ironed, food to be cooked, his cufflinks found, the perfunctory lover who scarcely notices what it is that he's fucking.

For the high-society mistress in the seventeenth century, the advantages were somewhat different: essentially, social and financial. Her lover would certainly expect to pay, in gifts or in cash, for her services (and, even once he'd finished with them, would provide a pension or a golden handshake); he would be quite happy to be seen with her in public and, should she chance to get pregnant, would usually acknowledge and support the child – and probably do quite a bit to further its education and career. A society so overt about its extramarital sex life had no pressing reason to attempt to conceal the side effects from the world.

On the other side of the sexual fence, there were married women themselves taking lovers. Most extravagant and famous among them was Catherine the Great of Russia – who, besides her minor affairs, had a dozen 'officially recognised' lovers. Some of these, such as Grigori Orlov, she had while still married to Peter III, a man not quite mentally stable. Having deposed this husband, however (and then, it's claimed, had him murdered), she spent the thirty-four years of her widowhood lavishing affection, money and jewels on such youths as the impecunious Guards officer Potemkin – whom, in the end, she made a prince, Field Marshal and Grand Admiral of the Black Sea.

On a more homely level, non-royal women were also enjoying extramarital flirtations and affairs – their opportunity greatly increased by the birth of the 'idle middle-class wife', a woman whose work was unnecessary to her husband's financial achievements and who, indeed, by her indolence, displayed those achievements to the world. Such women must still have feared pregnancy, of course, but mainly, now, for its physical effects. The cynicism of their social group, its refusal to take – or be seen to take – anything terribly seriously, meant that even paternity was an issue it wasn't *too* cool to pursue.

In short, with a bit of cunning and luck, it seems to have been quite possible for a woman in the seventeenth and eighteenth centuries – if she came from the right sort of class – to explore, express and enjoy her own sexuality. All the more so since sensual pleasure – which, in effect, means a greater concern with the sexual satisfiaction of women – was central to the concept of Gallantry.

Architecture, too, played its part. An increase in the number of private bedrooms – as distinct from one long sleeping corridor – meant that couples, married or otherwise, no longer needed to snatch furtive sex in the dark. Able to explore one another's bodies – even, perhaps, to discuss what they were doing – the sexes seem to have grown more aware of one another's constitution. Men rediscovered the function of the clitoris, apparently forgotten since Ovid's time. As de Mandeville wrote in 1724: 'All our late discoveries in anatomy can find no other use for the clitoris but to whet the female desire by its frequent erections.'

And in France, at least, the invention of the bidet, at some time during the seventeenth century, appears to have encouraged oral sex – a delight that must previously have had its drawbacks, since people of the period were not renowned for frequent or regular bathing. As the Earl of Rochester complained in the 1670s:

> Fair hasty nymph, be clean and kind
> And all my joys restore
> By using paper still behind
> And sponges for before.

Meanwhile, many women used this leisure, this access to education and culture, this comparative freedom of social behaviour to press for more *radical* changes. Lady Mary Wortley Montagu, born in 1689, was a political journalist whose *Letters* and *Woman Not Inferior to Man*

131

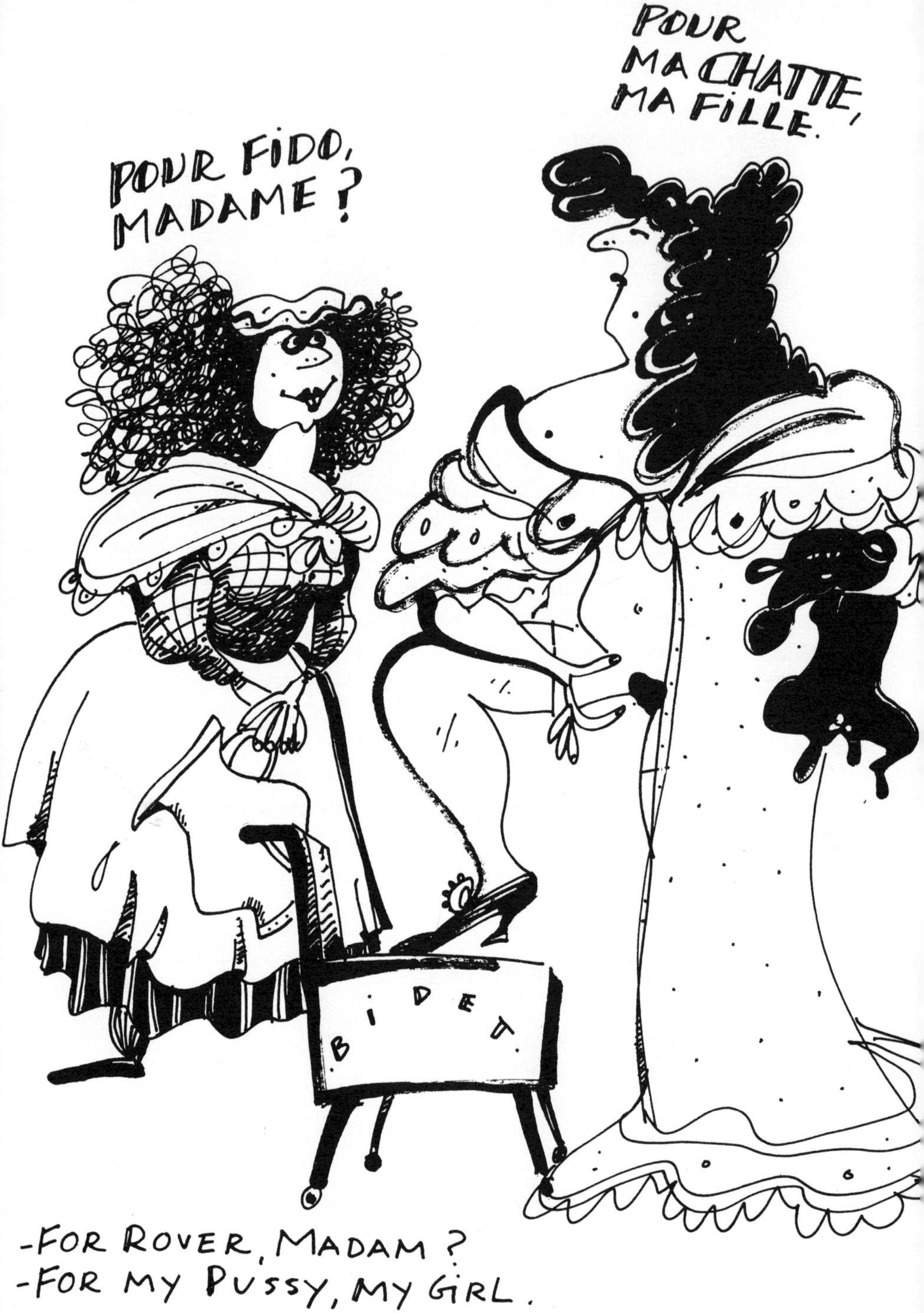

-FOR ROVER, MADAM?
-FOR MY PUSSY, MY GIRL.

promoted education for women as more advantageous than marriage. (While she was about it, she also introduced the smallpox inoculation to England.)

Another Mary, Mary de la Rivière Manley, was principally a dramatist – using her plays to expose such injustices as women's inordinate dependence on their 'good reputation' – but she also wrote political satires and novels and, in 1711, followed Jonathan Swift as editor of the *Examiner*. She also, perhaps most importantly, documented women's lives – and in *The Cabal*, one collection of such documents, wrote about lesbian lovers and suggested that women's sexual existence might well be improved without men.

Most of the women authors weren't specifically concerned with a woman's right to sexual satisfaction. What they were insisting, arguing, *proving* was that sexual inequality wasn't inherent – that, given male opportunities, women could equal male achievements. But the waves from this argument would eventually affect our sexual assumptions, self-image and behaviour far more profoundly than the fact that their contemporaries Elizabeth Foster, the Countess of Oxford and the Duchess of Devonshire were producing between them enough illegitimate children to furnish a school – refreshing though it is that they might do so and not be hanged, burned, stoned, or otherwise put to death.

And the writers did strike an answering chord in men – albeit a sad minority – in whom the Puritan-initiated concept of democracy was still at work. In 1694, yet another Mary, the writer and polemicist Mary Astell, wrote as follows: 'Women are from their very infancy debarred those advantages, with the want of which they are afterwards reproached, and nursed up in those vices which will hereafter be upbraided to them.' Four years later came this from Daniel (*Robinson Crusoe/Moll Flanders*) Defoe:

I have often thought of it as one of the most barbarous customs in the world, considering us a civilised and a Christian Country, that we deny advantages of learning to women. We reproach the sex every day with folly and impertinence: while I am confident, had they advantages of education equal to us, they would be guilty of less than ourselves.

I WILL NOT SAY VIRGINITY IS HAPPIER- BUT IT IS UNDOUBTEDLY SAFER THAN ANY MARRIAGE- IN A LOTTERY WHERE THERE ARE- AT THE LOWEST COMPUTATION- TEN THOUSAND BLANKS TO A PRIZE, IT IS THE MOST PRUDENT CHOICE NOT TO VENTURE-

LADY MARY WORTLEY MONTAGU

Natural woman

As the eighteenth century thrashed its way to those revolutions with which it would, in its closing years, erupt, there were many men who felt, like Defoe, that women should have some other education than the purely domestic, practical one to which they were largely confined.

The famous lexicographer and critic Dr Johnson – though renowned for his sneers at women who preached – was of the not unreasonable opinion that men who opposed education for women were frightened of being outstripped. Even that randy diarist Samuel Pepys was convinced that a woman might manage more than to plan a dinner for eight.

What prompted men in increasing numbers to think that women like the Marys might be right was finding themselves, in this age of abandon, so often in women's *company*. There, they discovered the astonishing fact that not only courtesans but other blokes' wives could be as funny, perceptive, shrewd, articulate and informed as themselves – and, in tandem, that women they'd previously thought to be intrinsically stupid were probably only suffering from lack of opportunity.

And since a lively, unoppressed mind can make anything – sex included – more fun, Zounds! they thought, what short-sighted fellows we've been.

Allies, then, such men as these, but not *entirely* to be counted on – their interests, inevitably, being first for themselves. Defoe, for instance (if only through having an eye to his future career), was quick to add to his plea that women be educated this rider: 'Not that I am for exalting the female government in the least. . . .'

Not to be counted on in any way at *all* – a man, in fact, whose influence does damage to women even now – was the French philosopher Jean-Jacques Rousseau (1712-1778). In some respects an interesting thinker, responsible as much as anyone else for the cry of 'Liberty! Equality! Fraternity!' soon to resound around the Western world, he too believed:

A MAN WHO *THINKS* SHOULD NOT ALLY HIMSELF WITH A WOMAN WHO DOES *NOT* THINK—

FOR HE LOSES THE CHIEF DELIGHT OF SOCIAL LIFE IF HE HAS A WIFE WHO CANNOT SHARE **HIS** THOUGHTS...

BUT i WOULD A *THOUSAND* TIMES HAVE A HOMELY GIRL THAN A LEARNED LADY... A FEMALE WIT IS A SCOURGE TO EVERYBODY—FROM THE LOFTY HEIGHTS OF HER GENIUS... SHE SCORNS EVERY WOMANLY DUTY—

And what were those womanly duties?

Why, surprise, surprise. They were to remain confined to the home, to devote herself to the comfort of her husband, to bear him children and to rear them. 'Her honour', as Rousseau so succinctly put it, 'is to be unknown; her glory is the respect of her husband; her joys the happiness of her family.'

This view was part of a general reaction to what M. Rousseau and many others saw as the decadence of Europe's high society – was part of an attempt to rediscover human beings' 'natural' virtues. If based on a good deal of wishful thinking, it did at least have the merit of providing an ideological alternative to the cynical, bugger-the-poor approach of those who nibbled each others' earlobes at Versailles, St James's Palace and St Petersburg.

But women, in particular, should always beware the word 'natural'. Dictionaries offer a dozen definitions (besides those specifically related to music, card games, theology, etc.) and it can, in fact, mean anything or nothing – except that, on most occasions when it's used, it will carry a note of approval. (In just the same way that 'unnatural' implies condemnation.)

So, when women are instructed to be 'natural' they are only being told to behave in a manner of which the speaker approves – except that the order is camouflaged by a word implying objectivity, implying that it makes no difference to the *speaker* how women insist on conducting themselves, but that, as a matter of objective fact, they'd be happier behaving as suggested.

And those things that Rousseau perceived as natural were women's sexual passivity, their desire for pregnancy and breastfeeding, their love of housekeeping, spinning and sewing, their gentleness, their respect for men's minds, their lack of the slightest desire of their own. . . .

Boring, boring, boring – were it not that Rousseau's philosophical approach, his insistence that all this was 'natural', added a new and alarming dimension to men's oppression of women – one especially suited to the age that was just then coming into being.

While notions of 'self' had been largely defined by the social group into which one was born and the fact of possessing one or other set of sexual organs – states, in other words, beyond one's control – 'identity' wasn't something about which too many people were worried. By the eighteenth century, however, with God, the monarchy and absolutes in general thrown wide open to question, to change, people were starting to feel more and more responsible for their 'selves'. And, since gender is such an important part of a person's identity – has, in any case, been made so – anyone told that they're being 'unnatural' in terms of their sexual behaviour is open to innumerable worries.

They are, in short, being tempted to perform their own oppression of themselves – to apply their *own* locks and chastity belts as defences against the loneliness of not knowing who they are.

Of course, there were women in Rousseau's time (just as before or since) who liked nothing better, at the end of the day, than to sit by the hearth with a child at their breast and a good meal stewing in the (polished) oven. The maternal bit in particular – the bearing, nurturing and rearing of children – is something which, along with the problems, can give phenomenal pleasure. But even for those who enjoy and enjoyed it, there ought to be a *choice* in the matter – not to mention the right to do other things as well – if only so that the role they've chosen isn't taken for granted and devalued.

In fact, Rousseau's bluff is resoundingly called by this sentence from his book *Emile*: 'They [women] must be trained to bear the yoke from the first, so that they may not feel it, to master their own caprices and to submit themselves to the will of others.' So much for nature, eh, Jean-Jacques?

Brotherhood

Rousseau's longed-for French Revolution finally took place in 1789. Six years earlier, America had sealed its own independence from Britain's king. And, in both cases, women had played a decisive part in the conflict.

In Paris, for instance, it had been in the salons of Mesdames Roland, Robert and de Genlis that Girondists, republicans and Orleanists shaped their political theories. More practically, it was a deputation composed entirely of women which invaded the famous Assembly at Versailles to return Louis XVI to Paris and the guillotine. 'The women,' wrote Michlet, 'were at the vanguard of our Revolution – one shouldn't be surprised, they were suffering even more than we were.'

Indeed. And as soon as the dust had settled – as soon, in America, as independence from Britain had been achieved; as soon, in France, as the National Convention had settled into its stride – they were left to continue with their suffering. No vote; few legal rights; few rights to personal property; the object of male desires and whims, valued (if at all) as mothers and housekeepers: in both Brave New Worlds, the position of women was either as bad as or worse than before. Well might the American Declaration of Independence pronounce: 'We hold these truths to be self-evident, that all *men* are created equal. . . .'

Revolutions for the rights of men do tend to be just what they say. In the more recent turmoils of the 1960s, women who gave their brains, hearts and bodies to Civil Rights, anti-Vietnam, anti-Gaullist and other revolutionary movements also realised that their 'radical' brothers valued them only as envelope-addressers; or sex objects. As the leading black activist Stokely Carmichael once, notoriously, declared: for a woman in the Student Non-Violent Coordinating Committee the only good position is 'prone'.

DÉCLARATION
DES DROITS DE L'HOMME
~~ET DU CITOYEN.~~

DE LA
CITOYENNE

The sexless woman

The year is 1837 and a new, young queen has ascended to the throne of Great Britain. But this one is no Gloriana – with one pale eye on the proud, pretty lords and another, still shrewder, on politics. Victoria Regina is scarcely more than a figurehead.

When she takes the crown, at the age of 18, it is the Prime Minister, Lord Melbourne, who guides her – and urges her to marry with the celebrated words: 'You'll be much more comfortable; for a woman cannot stand alone for long, in whatever situation she is.' So marry she does, two years later – proceeding to bear nine children. On the death of their father, Prince Albert, she withdraws into perpetual mourning.

Whether through inclination or not, Victoria became a symbol of her age: a devoted wife, a prolific mother, materially pampered, powerless. And, unlike Elizabeth I, Catherine the Great or Marie Antoinette, most definitely *not* a sex symbol. For almost two thirds of her reign, indeed, the image that she projected on her subjects was that described by Mary MacCarthy in *A Nineteenth Century Childhood*: 'an ancient Queen with bonnet strings and funereal black kid gloves, who drove daily in a landau to visit a mausoleum in her park.'

Any woman in the nineteenth century who needed to be seen to be 'respectable' – which, in effect, meant all but the poorest, those with nothing whatsoever to lose – was expected to behave in much the same fashion as her sovereign. For the era, despite its Imperial expansion, cut-throat trading, technological advances – or, quite possibly, because of these – was one of inordinate anxiety: one in which anything remotely 'unusual' was captured, catalogued and slammed under glass. Exotic animals were thrust into zoos, or killed, stuffed and presented to museums; flowers were dried of their juices and stood in glass domes. And women – as 'unusual' in the eyes of men as snow leopards or cheetahs – were forced by the legal and financial hold of their fathers, husbands, guardians or employers to appear, at least, to be 'ladies'.

Being a lady involved a lot of ludicrous, time-wasting practices, including the use of euphemisms for anything to do with the body and its functions. By taking this to absurd extremes, it was even decreed that piano legs – oops, I'm sorry, *legs* wasn't ladylike; piano *limbs* is what I should have written – must be covered to prevent offence.

But being a lady wasn't simply ridiculous. Its *central* requirement was that a woman de-sex herself; become not simply a person who didn't display her sexuality in public, but one who had no sexuality *at all*. This, to be precise, was the formula: 'A modest woman seldom desires any sexual gratification for herself. She submits to her husband, but only to please him; and, but for the desire of maternity, would far rather be relieved from his attention.'

'... 'NO NERVOUS YOUNG MAN NEED THEREFORE BE DETERRED. FROM MARRIAGE BY AN EXAGGERATED NOTION OF THE DUTIES REQUIRED OF HIM' _*

WILLIAM ACTON.

Curious, eh? Up to now, after all, it had been accepted that women's sexuality was either as great as or infinitely greater than men's. Their vaginas had been seen as insatiable mouths that could easily devour a poor penis; their clitorises as inexhaustible cravers of carnal pleasure. Even in the Romantic concept of women's sexual passivity, there was still the assumption that, once aroused, they felt as desirous as men.

Now, behold, that wasn't true at all: ladies were sexually null and void, while men (in another reversal) became the degenerate, uncontrollable, sexually incontinent beasts. And this is a theory that haunts us today – so much so, that we often don't realise how recently it came into being.

The effect of such thinking on marital sex can be imagined. The husband, if remotely sensitive, would be embarrassed by what he was doing to someone who 'would far rather be relieved from his attention' and finish it as fast as he could; or else, if devoid of empathy, would bang away like the uncontrollable ravager he thought himself to be. Even should a woman, incredibly, find herself starting to get aroused, feeling a desire for more of the same, or for something different, or for *anything*, she would have to deny the fact to herself or, if she couldn't, at least to her husband. To admit it would be to lose her one asset, her ladylikeness; would be to risk physical punishment, ostracism or penury.

Such enforced frustration – coupled with the lack of alternative, non-sexual outlets for their energy – was almost certainly the no. 1 reason why so many middle-class, Victorian women suffered interminable illnesses: depressions, declines, attacks of the vapours, even the notorious 'hysteria'.

Although it is now quite obvious why Victorian ladies, faced with a battery of nigh-on impossible commandments, had a tendency to get hysterical, their doctors were convinced that their emotional outbursts, their attacks of quite literal, physical paralysis, were caused by their *wombs* having got detached and having wandered off round their body.

Hence the name that they gave to the behaviour, from the same Greek root as hysterectomy – and hysterectomies were all too often the *cure* that they recommended.

Indeed, it was under the name of 'medicine' that women in the nineteenth century suffered some of the worst barbarities. Imagine this young Victorian wife, wealthy (in the sense that her *husband* is wealthy), intelligent, curious, good-natured and bored. She's been married for a couple of months or so and, as she lies on her chaise-longue, flicking through the pages of a fashion magazine, her mind traipses round the insoluble problem of why her tender, affectionate husband should, every time that he enters her bed, become transformed into a shifty stranger.

She knows that, being a woman, she can't be expected to understand what Sexual Lust is about, but still she fails to see why her husband can't at least kiss her, hold her, talk to her, be a bit *nice* to her while he Does It. She happens rather to like his body, the glimpses that she gets of his throat and his chest, the smell from his warm, damp skin. Thinking about it, her own body flushes with . . . what? Of course, she has no idea. So let's imagine that, unforewarned, ignorant of what she is doing, she starts to make love to herself.

Slam! She's now in a new sort of trouble. A moment ago, she was merely frustrated – destined, of course, to grow ever more angry, ever more bitter, unhappy, self-hating, but, precisely because of that, an exemplary Victorian woman: a woman like poor old Jane Carlyle, wife of the famous man of letters, Thomas, whose husband's refusal to accept her sexuality drove her to extremes of hypochondria – but now, whatever she chooses to do, our blushing bride is an outcast.

Perhaps only she will ever know what happened to her body as she stroked it. In that case, eaten by worry and shame, she will simply have to live with this horrible self-revelation as best she can.

Should she tell her husband, or should he find out, there's a chance, since he's quite well-intentioned, that he'll urge her to rest even more. But this, predictably, not having dampened her body's now-aroused sexuality, he might then take her to a doctor – and there's where our woman's nightmare becomes waking hell.

For the doctor – that stern, male authority on what women feel and what not – is likely to prescribe that our young wife be *shackled* whenever she's alone in her bed, might even provide some degrading, painful version of handcuffs for the purpose. Besides what this is likely to do for her own confusion and uncertainties, one can just imagine how it will affect her husband's attitude towards her. Worse, the doctor may suggest that our wife have 'a little operation'; bluntly – though the doctor *himself* won't be blunt; may even, if his name is Isaac Barker Brown, tell the couple an outright lie – the surgical removal of her clitoris.

We Westerners tend to assume that 'clitoridectomy' has only been practised by certain Muslim and tribal African societies. Certainly, in those, it continues: on reaching puberty, a young woman will either have the tip of her clitoris cut off, the entire organ, or even, occasionally, the labia (the lips) round her vagina. She may also suffer infibulation, in which, her clitoris and labia removed, the mouth of her vagina will be sewn together. This deliberate truncating of a woman's sexuality has, in the East, acquired a ceremonial importance, is considered to be a rite of passage from girlhood to adult womanhood. But the practice, though much more whispered and covert, was also rife in the Victorian West, a favourite resort of those specialists in women's 'disorders'. In fact, as recently as *1948*, a 5-year-old girl in the USA was given a clitoridectomy to 'cure' her of masturbation.

Where female bodies insist on behaving in ways that men say they shouldn't, it's the bodies, not men's opinions, that tend to get cut down to size.

As we've seen, it wasn't merely clitorises that got butchered. Wombs were sliced out at the drop of a hat – and not only from women who cried and/or laughed to what was considered excess, but from any woman suspected of having 'simple hysterical mania'. And all that was needed to suffer from that was to become 'rapidly less and less conventional. Thus a lady will smoke, talk slang, or be extravagant in dress; and will declare her intention of doing as she likes.'

Beyond the drawing room

The hell of being a Victorian lady was balanced – indeed, could only exist – by the co-existence of a hell where women were 'scrubbers', 'hussies' and prostitutes.

Sometimes, these worlds were divided by nothing but the green baize door to the servants' quarters, where parlourmaids, chambermaids, tweenies and slaveys – women whose only alternative was to find themselves, penniless, out on the street – were often subjected to the Lust that their masters preferred not to show to their wives; or (more commonly still, it would seem) were sexually abused by their employers' sons: boys and young men impatient with waiting for their long engagements (to virgins) to end.

Simultaneously, Victorian menfolk fled to the brothels in droves. So great was their demand for prostitutes that even their regular supplier – the massive, urban poverty on which prosperity swam – couldn't keep filling the orders. Kidnapping, the 'white slave trade', became an alternative source – one doubly needed because of the novel requirement for *virgin* prostitutes.

What else, after all, could allow a man to express his 'natural beastliness' while, at the same time, placing in his arms the perfect woman of his era. That she'd got there by being abducted, drugged, tricked or threatened with violence, what did he care about that? The very fact that he'd found her in a brothel made her, *per se*, no lady.

Often, she wasn't even a woman. Girls from 14 to 18 years old could be purchased for £20 (or, if from a middle-class background, for up to £100), while an upper-class 12-year-old virgin could be bought for £500 – a sum which becomes even more grotesque if you think that, in 1880, a working family was likely to earn a total of £1.50 a week. 'Used' prostitutes frequently had their vaginas stitched tighter again – an operation which, painful in itself, could also lead to severe laceration when next the woman (or child) was penetrated.

150

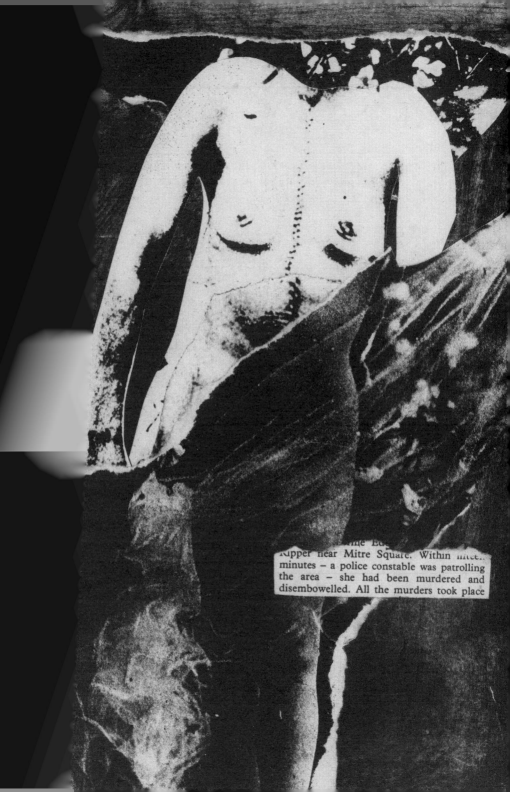

...the Ed...
...ipper near Mitre Square. Within mfee...
minutes – a police constable was patrolling
the area – she had been murdered and
disembowelled. All the murders took place

These outrages became so excessive, even within their own context, that, in 1885, a four-part exposé was run in the London paper the *Pall Mall Gazette*. The relevations caused such a sensation that copies were selling at twelve times their usual price – even though W.H. Smith, the newsagents, refused to touch the distribution – and the articles were subsequently syndicated in the USA and brought out in book form in Paris.

Their author, it transpired, had been less than factually scrupulous, which led to his being sued and imprisoned, but there was quite enough truth in his stories for the shock to carry on reverberating – and to be used by a pressure group, the National Association, to crown its campaign against the abuse of prostitutes.

The National Association had been started in 1869 in response to the Contagious Diseases Act (1864). This latter was a parliamentary move designed to curtail the spread of venereal disease, but which, in practice, merely succeeded in terrorising working-class women, subjecting any who were out on the street to arbitrary and compulsory medical inspection; an inefficient, unhygienic procedure that was quite as likely to *infect* a woman as to spot that she was already infected. Found 'guilty' of infection, a woman was likely to be detained in a Lock Hospital (more emphasis on Lock than Hospital) and, on release, to find herself officially registered a prostitute – effectively ensuring that, whether or not that was what she had been, henceforth that was what she would remain. (Men's role in the spread of VD, meanwhile, was totally disregarded.)

Formed to oppose this practice, the National Association had a significantly large, important and active membership of independent women – the writer Harriet Martineau, the nursing pioneer Florence Nightingale, the feminist activist Josephine Butler – middle-class women who were daring to nudge at the limits of ladylike behaviour. They were reviled in the press: 'frenzied, unsexed and utterly without shame'. They were physically attacked at their public meetings. But, by the latter half of the century, their numbers had grown too vast for them *all* to be punished as 'simple hysterical maniacs' or sluts. Following the *Pall Mall Gazette*'s exposé, a petition was delivered to Parliament that was signed by 393,000 people. Unrolled, it stretched for two miles. Reform became unavoidable. The Contagious Diseases

Act was repealed, the age of consent was raised to 16, brothels were made subject to police raids, and there were stricter regulations on soliciting.

Needless to say, the exploitation of prostitutes didn't just stop. Indeed, ironically, in many ways their life was now more of a hassle, for the middle-class women who had fought on their behalf had done so primarily so that their sisters could live the same 'virtuous' lives as themselves – had, in effect, been demanding that everyone join them in sexual exile.

Controlling birth

When contraception emerged as an issue for late nineteenth-century women activists, it has to be said that even *that* wasn't primarily (or even at all) as a means of increasing a woman's chances of sexual pleasure and fulfilment. It was seen far more as a means of reducing poverty – or, to be precise, of reducing the poor, so that there might be fewer of them to share the crumbs they were allowed.

The concept of sexual freedom was a lot less likely to strike a woman *then* as something to be promoted. But perhaps more important in making contraception an economic (as distinct from a sexual) issue in the late nineteenth century was the fact that the debate had originated with men. It was a male economist, Malthus, whose *Essay on the Principle of Population* (1798) had started the whole thing off.

This isn't to say that women hadn't been trying to prevent conception for centuries – not to 'control the population' but to try to preserve their battered, individual bodies. If men wouldn't contemplate abstinence, or sexual alternatives to intercourse, then *something* had to be attempted.

The Ancients tended to place their faith in amulets, magic jewellery – and, when those failed to have any effect, would sometimes have their stomachs massaged by a friendly neighbourhood 'wisewoman' in an effort to promote an abortion. If the worst came to the worst, it was not uncommon for infants simply to be exposed to the elements (it wasn't until the fourth century AD that the Romans expressly forbade this), but, where possible, women obviously favoured pre-emptive action.

Besides wearing amulets, Roman women had a range of ingenious ploys. One was simply to hold their breath at the moment their partner ejaculated. Another, *rather* more likely to work, was to stuff their vaginas with honey-soaked wool. The more sophisticated even followed a 'rhythm' method of birth control – trying to avoid sexual intercourse on those days when they were most likely to conceive – but its value was somewhat undermined by the Roman belief that a woman was at her most fertile just after she'd menstruated.

Still, throughout the Middle Ages, the Renaissance and the seventeenth and eighteenth centuries, women were attempting to counteract the effects of men's sexual self-centredness – their efforts assisted and, by and large, made less disastrous than they might have been by 'wisewomen', 'old wives' or midwives: these local healers so much more in tune with women's bodies and experience than doctors. And all of this had largely been private and personal, what knowledge there was being whispered from woman to woman: a matter of pragmatic, short-term need as distinct from a long-term national concern.

Malthus's book made the argument public, by suggesting that the poor ought to marry much later so as not to outgrow their resources. Picking up on its central idea, James Mill, another economist, hinted at more *efficient* methods for checking poor people's birth rate. The early radicals switched the emphasis away from *controlling* the numbers of the poor to allowing the poor to control their numbers *themselves*. The newspaper *The Republican* began giving contraceptive information. It recommended the vaginal sponge – literally, a quinine-soaked sponge to be inserted into the vagina – and an early, far-from-featherweight sheath called the 'skin'. And books with titles like *Moral Physiology*, *Fruits of Philosophy*, *The Bridal Gem*, were published with the same information.

This dissemination of knowledge was not unopposed. The establishment was terrified of anything that gave the poor power, while many of the poorer men themselves saw in it a threat to their daughters' purity – or, more shrewdly, a distraction from the need to redistribute the nation's resources. And, if the arguments and counter-arguments have a familiar ring, it's probably because an identical debate still rages in relation to the Third World.

CONTRACEPTION

for whom?

FOR what?

FOR SOME, A THREAT TO WOMEN'S VIRTUE — ANOTHER MALE TRICK TO GET THEIR WAY

FOR OTHERS, A DISTRACTION FROM THE NEED TO REDISTRIBUTE THE NATION'S WEALTH.

By the late nineteenth century, middle-class women were in a position to enter the fray. Though still shackled by their ladyhood, they had too much information, education, energy and time not to tug at the restraints. Besides those women who had agitated for an end to the Contagious Diseases Act, there were middle-class feminists pushing for votes for women, for charitable homes for unmarried mothers and for better conditions for women industrial workers.

Such feminists' reaction to birth control was, to say the least, ambivalent. Enmeshed still in notions of 'virtue', they couldn't help seeing any innovation that might make sex more pleasant, or easy, as a threat to what they held sacred.

In 1877, the reformer Annie Besant and a colleague, Charles Bradlaugh, arranged to publish a cheap edition of one of the pro-contraception books – Charles Knowlton's *Fruits of Philosophy*. For this, Besant was arrested and charged with having published an obscene work, one that might suggest to the young and unmarried 'that they might gratify their passion'. Or, to quote the Solicitor General, 'a dirty, filthy book . . . the object of it is to enable persons to have sexual intercourse, and not to have that which in the order of Providence is the natural result of that sexual intercourse'. Let off, in the end, on a technical point, Annie Besant still lost the custody of her daughter through this action: the judge thought that the child might be influenced to follow in her mother's footsteps.

Crusaders like Besant were handicapped by the fact that mechanical contraception was still unreliable and awkward. Besides the vaginal sponge and the 'skin', there were really only vaginal syringes, through which a woman was supposed to sloosh her cunt with a mixture of alum and water.

From the 1870s onward, a few lucky women were able to lay their hands on a Dutch cap – originally called the Mensinga diaphragm, but nicknamed in honour of its doctor-inventor's nationality. But even the cap (as any woman who's worn one recently will know) is not the *simplest* of devices. Fairly reliable it may be – inserted high up in the vagina, it forms an effective rubber barrier to the entrance of the womb itself – but what is essentially a circular spring with a dome of rubber stretched over it can take quite a bit of manoeuvring; especially since it's usually suggested that the whole contraption be smothered in spermicidal jelly. Chasing one across the bathroom floor does tend to deflate sexual tension; it must often have punctured it as flat as a pancake for women who were even less at home with their bodies, their sexuality, than we are.

War and peace

The carnage of the First World War spattered blood, mud and doubt into everybody's eyes; but perhaps the assumptions most thoroughly disturbed belonged to those women who, as war broke out, were emerging from Victorian schoolrooms.

Suddenly, those friends of their brothers who would, had all gone according to plan, have danced with them and courted them and treated them as pure, silly creatures, were donning uniforms, sailing abroad and having their arms, legs, heads and guts plastered all over the earth. The convenient pretence that 'nice girls didn't' – didn't even want to, until they were married – was dropped as though it were a hand grenade. And the girls, their internalised restraints undone by a mixture of sentimental patriotism, horror and genuine pity, were all too willing to collude.

The writer Vera Brittain – who, in *Testament of Youth*, told of her passionate wartime love for an officer eventually slaughtered – explained what happened like this: 'For the younger generation life had grown short, and death was always imminent; the postponement of love to a legal occasion might mean its frustration for ever.'

More practically women were freed from their families' supervision. From having been told that their only value was as 'angels in the house' and as mothers, it now transpired that they were urgently needed to fill those peacetime posts left empty by men being shipped to their deaths. As secretaries and clerical workers, probably living away from home, they were in a *position* to comfort those boys on their way to Ypres or the Somme – acquiring confidence simultaneously as sexual beings and as workers.

Most profoundly affected of all were those women who went to the front with the VAD or the WAAC: women who nursed and drove ambulances, who witnessed the deaths, not only of soldiers but also of their volunteer sisters. If, for the 'ladies' among them, it ripped to

160

tatters any last thoughts that modesty, innocence and helplessness might be desirable, for all of them it opened the gates to belief in their own abilities and (no less importantly) to faith in those of other women.

Barbara 'Troupie' Lowther, for instance, a daughter of the sixth Earl of Lonsdale, formed her *own* ambulance unit, with a friend, and took it right up to where the French army was fighting at the Front at Compiègne. Her drivers included not only British but also French and American women – who, between them, ferried thousands of wounded men to the dressing stations (and five of whom were awarded the Croix de Guerre). In a post-war interview in *The Times*, Troupie declared it 'a wonderful time. We were often 350 yards from the German lines awaiting the wounded, under camouflage.' The American writer Gertrude Stein, living as an expatriate in France, also drove an ambulance.

The end of the war brought a halt to such obvious 'adventures', but it did see a number of concrete improvements in women's social condition. British women achieved the vote (in 1918 for those over 30, in 1928 on the same terms as men), became entitled to hold public office, civil posts and judicial posts, and were also, if householders, free to be members of juries – so long, that is, as the case being tried wasn't of a sexual nature: in which case, the judge would discreetly cough and the women were expected to leave.

In 1923, moreover, British women could sue for divorce on the grounds (always open to their husbands) of adultery – and, in 1932, those who were married got the right to control of their property.

The Nineteenth Amendment to the US Constitution gave American women the vote in 1920; German women had won the right a few days after the war ended; in Canada and Belgium, by some twist of logic, the vote was only awarded, at first, to the widows and mothers of war casualties; while, in France, women's suffrage wouldn't come until 1944. But all through the West women voters were slowly, inexorably, becoming the rule.

More informally, women's attitudes to sex had been altered for good. An increasing number – both of public figures and private individuals – were involved in discussions on birth control, the rights of unmarried mothers, reform of the laws concerning abortion and, conspicuously, sexual *pleasure*.

161

HELL'S ANGELS
Howard Hughes'
Thrilling
Multi-Million
Dollar-Air
Spectacle
with
JEAN
HARLOW
Ben Lyon
James Hall
UNITED
ARTISTS
PICTURE

Marie Stopes, for instance, who established the first British birth control clinic in 1921, was not just promoting contraception as an economic imperative, but as part of a woman's right to have carefree sexual intercourse. Indeed, in her best-selling book *Married Love*, published in 1918, she even dared to suggest that, during the time that a woman was pregnant, intercourse might well be replaced by some other form of sexual stimulation. Of course, she aroused both anger and outrage – to the extent that, in 1924, *The Times* of London refused to publish an announcement of her daughter's birth – but she also got hundreds of letters from women asking her for advice and, in her answers, urged them on to expect much more from their sex lives. Calling orgasms 'wonderful tides', she was far removed in her aims and assumptions from those who had fought, in the nineteenth century, for all women's right to be chaste.

The Russian politician and writer Alexandra Kollontai, who'd helped to shape the 1917 Bolshevik revolution, saw 'free love' as a necessary part of Communism's new order. A woman should feel and be free to have sex, whether married or not, with whomever she chose.

The British thinker Dora Russell agreed: women had a right to sexual *enjoyment*. In her book *Hypatia* (1925) she looked at what women had achieved to date and expressed her hopes for their future:

> We went as far as we dared with an eye to male hostility. Young feminists today would be the first to admit that it would probably have paid us to go further.... To me the important task of modern feminism is to accept and proclaim sex: to bury for ever the lie that the body is a hindrance to the mind, and sex a necessary evil to be endured for the perpetuation of our race.

Even as they expressed it, however, the thinking of women such as Stopes, Kollontai and Russell was being hijacked. As it increased in popularity, the establishment started to accept it; but channelled it away from its logical conclusion – that a woman's sex life need not, if she chooses, have anything at all to do with childbirth – towards the idea that certainly, yes, a woman should have a good sex life, but that the pinnacle of all this pleasure, its greatest fulfilment . . .

AFTER ALL — it's ONLY NATURAL —

MARY X YEARNED FOR MOTHERHOOD — YET — AFTER YEARS OF FUCKING IN MANY WEIRD AND WONDERFUL WAYS WITH A VARIETY OF PARTNERS — SHE STILL HADN'T CONCEIVED —

BUT FORTUNATELY THERE WERE OPTIONS — ALL WAS NOT **LOST** FOR MARY X.

ARTIFICIAL INSEMINATION   TEST TUBE

Concerning pricks

For centuries, men had been telling women what their sexuality meant, how it worked and what they should feel about it. And even now that large numbers of women were publicly debating the matter themselves – bringing to it, as men could not, their personal, first-hand experience – male voices would keep interrupting and trying to shift the discussion their way.

At the very beginning of the century – precisely in 1900 – a book had been published called *Die Traumdeutung* (*The Interpretation of Dreams*): the work of a Viennese doctor, Sigmund Freud, who received a number of polite reviews but who didn't, at the time, create very much public sensation.

In the years that followed the First World War, however, his ideas began to spread – until there was scarcely a person who didn't, however vaguely, know about 'traumas', 'repression', 'the unconscious', etc. Newspapers, novels and women's magazines all became soaked in Freudianism (if often diluted, or adulterated) as did the casual chit-chat of people in trains, living rooms and bars.

One of Freud's central concerns was with human sexuality – indeed, he saw it as the force behind all that we do – and, of course, he had a lot to say on the nature of *female* sexuality. Rejecting the accepted beliefs of his time – that any woman who was sexually demanding needed her clitoris or womb knifed out – he insisted that it was natural for women to be sexual beings: not only that, but that it was important that their sexuality functioned correctly. The trouble began with how he perceived that functioning.

Freud saw human sexuality in general as passing through a series of stages. First, he believed, comes the 'oral' stage, in which our desires are centred on our mouth and gratified by breastfeeding, sucking, tasting, and eating everything we come across. Next, he thought, comes the 'anal' stage, in which shitting and asses are the centre of erotic interest. And third comes the stage known as 'phallic', when our focus shifts to our genital organs – in boys, the sensations in their penis, in girls, the sensations in their clitoris.

Now pivotal to Freud's beliefs about female sexuality was that it was absolutely vital for women (however difficult the process might be – and he did believe it could be difficult) to stop, at puberty, from concentrating on the sexual power of the clitoris and to switch to vaginal sexuality; in other words, to thoughts of sexual intercourse and, as the final fulfilment, pregnancy. *Whatever* a woman did sexually, he thought, was in compensation for not possessing that wonderful toy, a penis – it was he who invented the concept of women suffering from 'penis envy' – but whereas the clitoris as compensation was infantile, was 'childish masculinity', a stage that had to be passed through, creating a *child* as compensation was mature, correct, desirable.

The male-centredness of this view, its assumption that women's behaviour is shaped by their failure to be like men (as distinct from their palpable success in being like women), was mainly due to the fact that Freud arrived at most of his conclusions not from observing the behaviour of others but from contemplating his own. When wondering how a woman operated, he could therefore only wonder how he *himself* would operate without a penis – and compensation, from that point of view, was not an unreasonable answer.

Very few women, however, have any desire for a penis. They may think it might be useful to have one to piss from; otherwise, what they usually 'envy' is all the freedom, power and prestige that having a penis seems to confer. Kate Millett made this point in *Sexual Politics* (1970) and, moreover, pointed out that children are likely to notice breasts as desirable long before penises. But Freud was not in the habit of asking his patients – male or female – what they wanted. Rhetorically he was famous for enquiring, 'What do women want?'; in practice he preferred to tell them.

And, in any case, women who, for the better part of a century, had had it drummed into their heads that they were sexually non-existent were probably far too unsure of themselves to argue with such an authority.

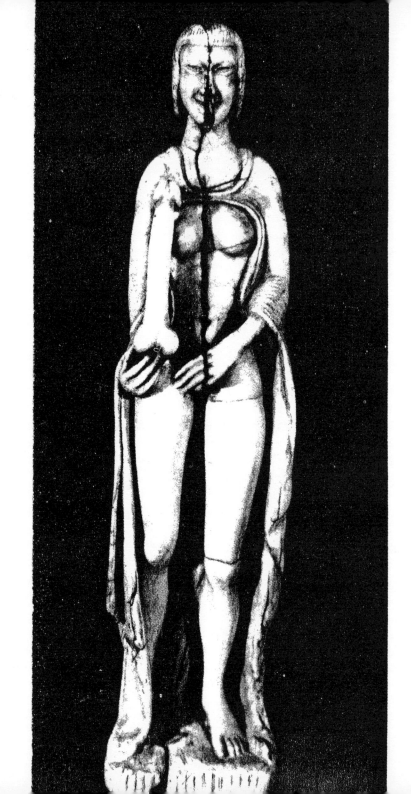

So now, as women in America and Europe were finally loosening the Victorian shackles, the dangers of staying 'mannish', of failing to progress beyond the stage of wanting to be like the boys, was slickly being poured into their ears.

And now, as contraception was slowly becoming a real possibility, it was being suggested that motherhood was all that prevented a woman going mad.

And now, as women were making inroads in public and professional life, a voice was warning them of terrible dangers to their children's future sanity if their mother wasn't continually beside them to protect them from infantile trauma.

None of this is to suggest that Freud was part of some massive conspiracy to ensure that women were as trapped as ever they had been: confined to passive and largely unpleasurable sex lives; encouraged to be mothers regardless of their wants; caught in enforced domesticity. Indeed, the present-day feminist Juliet Mitchell argued (in 1974) in favour of studying his theories:

> The greater part of the feminist movement has identified Freud as the enemy. It is held that psychoanalysis claims women are inferior and that they can achieve true femininity only as wives and mothers. . . . However . . . psychoanalysis is not a recommendation *for* a patriarchal society, but an analysis *of* one. If we are interested in understanding and challenging the oppression of women, we cannot afford to neglect it.

What Mitchell says makes a good deal of sense, but Freud's implications of women's inferiority, his suggestions that women 'can achieve true femininity only as wives and mothers', were certainly leapt on as *recommendations* by many who wanted to believe them. And they continue, as I said before, to stain our everyday thinking. Here, as late as 1973, is the British MP Leo Abse on women who presume to enter politics:

> Is Freud correct in his deductive assertion that the discovery that she is 'castrated' is a turning point in a girl's growth? Are many of our women politicians the little girls who refused to recognise the unwelcome fact that they lacked a penis and, defiantly rebellious, exaggerated their masculinity?

FREUDIAN SLIP.

Slightly less influential than Freud, but still a man whose theories were having an impact on women post-First World War was the curious British sexologist Havelock Ellis. Ellis – whose wife, Edith Less, was lesbian – had written, in 1897, what was perhaps the first serious study of male and female homosexuality: a book called *Sexual Inversion*. In it, he had at least tried to argue against his contemporaries' conviction that 'homosexuals' were either mentally unbalanced or evil – so that, by the 1920s, 'enlightened' people had come to accept that 'dykes' and 'queers' didn't necessarily need locking up.

The trouble was that Ellis's theories were no less absurd than his predecessors' – and led to some commonly held beliefs of tear-inducing stupidity. His very use of the word 'invert' to describe a homosexual person, for instance, indicated his profound conviction that homosexual men were 'feminine' men and homosexual women 'masculine' women. These congenitally abnormal people were, he insisted, capable of doing great, good works in their communities – but, since the 'true invert' woman, for example, could only be attracted to a 'feminine' woman (one, in other words, who really should be with a *man*), she was doomed to emotional misery.

Today, when such theories are put forward, lesbian women are in a position to tell their authors what to do with them. In the years that followed the First World War, even a woman brave enough to try would almost certainly have found herself crushed into silence.

Breaking the silence

The silence of lesbian women throughout vast tracts of our history is resounding. Women have certainly loved other women, as we've seen, since the earliest times. Until the rise of Athens as the dominant Ancient Greek city-state, they celebrated quite openly their emotional and physical desires. But then, for centuries, their voices got muffled to the point of virtual extinction – partly by the repressiveness of church and state legislation on sex and partly by women's general exclusion from mainstream writing, painting and most other art forms.

Those written works and pictures that tell us of lesbianism's continued existence, from the time of Sappho to the twentieth century, are almost exclusively the products of men: of authors like the Marquis de Sade, who, at the turn of the eighteenth century, wrote about lesbian sex among prostitutes; or visual artists such as Henry Fuseli – at one time a lover of the feminist writer Mary Wollstonecraft – who, in the early nineteenth century, sketched several pictures of women friends in casually erotic embraces.

One rare exception, as we've already seen, was Mary de la Rivière Manley's documentation of lesbian love in her eighteenth-century book *The Cabal* – though even that wasn't (overtly, at least) a firsthand, personal account. Indeed, most women of the period would have been decidedly hesitant to rock the boat. As the present-day writer Lillian Faderman has argued in *Surpassing the Love of Men*, lesbian sex was probably condoned so long as it kept itself terribly quiet. So long as women 'appeared feminine, their sexual behaviour would be viewed as an activity in which women indulged when men were unavailable or as an apprenticeship or appetite-whetter to heterosexual sex.'

Today, quite a number of 'ordinary' housewives, indistinguishable from their neighbours, are having or have had affairs with other

174

women: something in the region of 9 per cent, according to the mid-1960s research of Americans John Gagnon and William Simon; probably more than one in ten, according to *The Woman Book of Love and Sex*, a survey of 15,000 British women conducted by Deirdre Sanders *et al.* in 1983. And this is an age when other people's knowing about one's lesbianism is not, for all the problems it can cause, the inevitable end of the world. In past ages, with church and state on the sniff for *any* sex that wasn't reproductive, women were even more likely than now to play down their lesbian relationships. Nor was it altogether difficult, since touching, kissing, holding and loving have graciously been permitted to women as part of their 'natural' self-expression.

By the end of the First World War, however, with women beginning to come to terms with their sexual desires and requirements, the subject of lesbianism was taken from ice. It was discussed in the radical journal *Freewoman* and, it appears, by feminists up and down the country. 'Among our friends,' wrote Vera Brittain, 'we discussed sodomy and lesbianism with as little hesitation as we compared the merits of different contraceptives. . . .'

'Our friends', of course, were a limited bunch – though apparently there were enough of them to get the authorities worried. In 1921 they attempted (albeit unsuccessfully) to make lesbian sex, for the first time ever, the subject of criminal law. (The Criminal Law Amendment Act of 1885, which had been the first British legislation against homosexual practice *per se*, ignored the existence of lesbian sex because, legend has it, dear Queen Victoria refused to believe women *did* such a thing.)

Then, in 1928, the authorities themselves made lesbianism the talk of anyone able to buy, or borrow, a daily newspaper. That summer, a popular novelist called Radclyffe Hall had published a rather turgid book entitled *The Well of Loneliness*: the story of a woman called Stephen who is 'cursed' by being born lesbian. It ends in all kinds of misery and gloom – not just for Stephen but those other 'inverts' whom she meets in her exile in Paris – and with the plea: 'Acknowledge us, oh God, before the whole world. Give us also the right to our existence.' The *Sunday Express* campaigned for its suppression – 'I would rather give a healthy boy or a healthy girl a phial of prussic acid than this novel' – and a highly publicised obscenity trial ensured that its subject matter was discussed by a far wider public than Vera Brittain's friends.

A number of prominent literary figures agreed to testify, in court, on behalf of *The Well*. Among them were Virginia Woolf, Rose Macaulay, E.M. Forster, A.P. Herbert, Desmond McCarthy and Storm Jameson. Many, not thinking the book very *good*, were a bit ambivalent at doing so. Storm Jameson even went rushing round to consult with Virginia Woolf on the matter, asking her whether they would have to swear that the book was a great piece of literature. 'No,' replied Virginia gravely, 'there will be no need for that.' But still, unlike Rebecca West, John Galsworthy and Evelyn Waugh (all of whom were approached and declined), they were at least enough incensed by the 'censorship' issue to agree. And all of them behaved with more courage than sexologist Havelock Ellis – whose theories, the discerning reader will have noticed, were dear to Radclyffe Hall's heart, and who had even contributed an introduction to her book. 'I *never* have been in the witness box,' he wriggled when asked if he'd testify. 'I do not possess the personal qualities that make a good witness. . . .'

The trial resulted in the book's being banned in Great Britain. It was later tried for obscenity, and found not guilty, in the United States. Sales were only affected for the good, reaching tens of thousands in fourteen countries – so that Radclyffe Hall was flooded with letters of gratitude from lesbian women, who felt that she was helping them to achieve their acknowledgment 'before the whole world'.

Their view, however, most certainly wasn't shared by all of their sisters. The lesbian writer Vita Sackville-West – with whom Virginia Woolf had a teasing, ambiguous sexual affair – said that *The Well* showed more than ever that 'a really good novel remains to be written on that subject'. The American painter Romaine Brooks dismissed *The Well* as 'a ridiculous book, trite, superficial, as was to be expected'. While another lover of Vita Sackville-West, the socialite Violet Trefusis, called it a 'loathsome example'.

All of them were angry at being represented (if only by strong association) as stereotypical 'butches' and 'femmes' – women who, in order to love other women, ape heterosexual behaviour, with one of them dressing and acting like a man and the other like a 'silly little woman'. They were also (perhaps even more) annoyed at being depicted as miserable as hell.

178

And they did have a point. Both Virginia Woolf's *Orlando* – a hymn of praise to Vita and androgeny also published in 1928 – and Gertrude Stein's 1914 *Tender Buttons* – egalitarian 'still-lifes' of love – were, in their different ways, too obscure to impress the popular imagination. For years to come, the *Well*'s would be the established image of lesbianism: a doomed condition, inherent from childhood, participated in either by women who couldn't get a 'real man' or by those unable, try as they might, to be a 'real woman' like the rest of us. The love that dared not speak its name might, after centuries, have done so – but guardians of motherhood and family values didn't need to start panicking. On the contrary, they'd just acquired a wonderful bogeywoman.

Pretty as a picture

Images are important. Radclyffe Hall, as we've only just seen, had largely adopted Havelock Ellis's image of the 'true invert'. Perhaps, had she never read *Sexual Inversion*, she'd still have decided to cut her hair short, wear a monocle and sink herself in misery. Perhaps she would still have treated her lovers as though they were archetypal wives. On the other hand, we have little indication that lesbian women *before* Havelock Ellis felt the need to exhibit such 'masculine' behaviour. The women on Lesbos certainly didn't; nor did those women arousing each other in Henry Fuseli's early nineteenth-century drawings.

But, by the middle of the twentieth century, as the world once again erupted into war, the Butch/Femme image of lesbian couples was established as the primary model. Gertrude Stein, the American Paris-based writer and patron of the arts, wore skirts and was barely 5 foot tall; but when, in middle age, she cut her hair short, she was stereotyped as 'masculine' – while Alice B. Toklas, a talented and strong-minded woman, became her 'wifely' lover. What made images so much more powerful as the twentieth century progressed was the growth in influence of newspapers, magazines, radio and the cinema – and, most of all, from the end of the Second World War, the influence of television.

Men, like women, are bombarded by media images: the Courageous Soldier, the Smooth City Gent, the Bohemian Hard-Drinking Artist. What's different about the images from which a woman's encouraged to choose is that they are almost exclusively concerned with sex – or, more precisely, with ways in which women might relate, as sexual beings, to men. That archetypal lesbian image was never intended to be *positive*. It was more in the way of a warning, a threat. Its assumption by lesbian women themselves was often, in fact, a defiant response to heterosexual sneerings and jeerings.

180

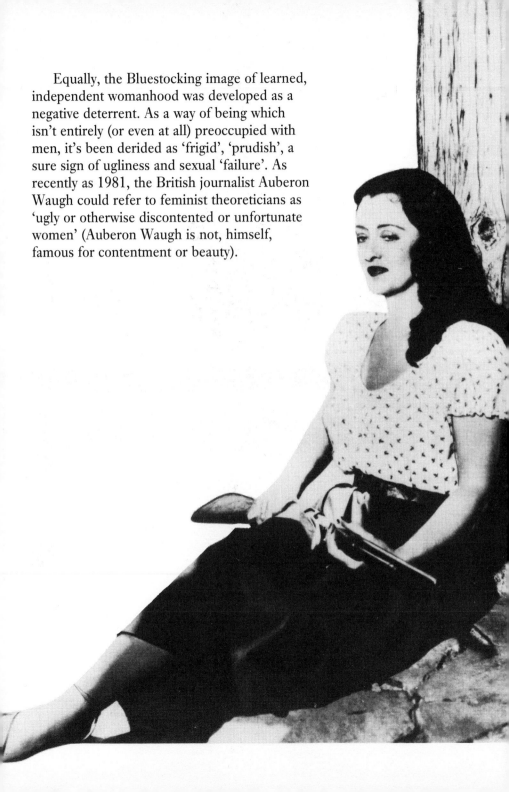

Equally, the Bluestocking image of learned, independent womanhood was developed as a negative deterrent. As a way of being which isn't entirely (or even at all) preoccupied with men, it's been derided as 'frigid', 'prudish', a sure sign of ugliness and sexual 'failure'. As recently as 1981, the British journalist Auberon Waugh could refer to feminist theoreticians as 'ugly or otherwise discontented or unfortunate women' (Auberon Waugh is not, himself, famous for contentment or beauty).

183

In post-war films, the Bluestocking was usually led to see the error of her ways. She'd begin the film as an ace reporter, a top librarian or a secretary, for instance, dressed as befitted her hard-working life, bespectacled and (as likely as not) played by Katherine Hepburn. Her attitude towards the film's hero would range from aggression to blithe disregard and most of the story would zing along fine on the – usually – highly erotic force of a courtship between equal adults. But, by the final frame of the movie, our heroine's horn-rimmed specs would be off, her hair shaken loosely all over her face and her job given up for the promise of marital extinction. And the film would be classed not as tragedy, but as a Romantic Comedy. (Needless to say, in the real post-war world, women who'd once again been allowed to run the factories and offices of wartime were being chivvied back into kitchens, nurseries, financial dependence, silence.)

Far more acceptable to men than either the Butch or the Bluestocking image – the first of which implies their redundancy, the second their disposability – are images such as the Scarlet Woman or the good old Tart with a Heart; or, at the other end of the scale, the Pure Young Virgin and the Nurturing Mother. The latter two, as we've already seen, were once combined in the Virgin Mary – a figure who, in the rather more secular 1940s, 1950s and 1960s, became transformed into the Girl Next Door.

Epitomised by many of the characters played by the film actor Doris Day, this improbable person was usually feisty, witty, a regular handful, but sexual purity (not to mention health, cleanliness and good, white teeth) was also essential to her being. She was, in effect, a charming little tomboy – who was destined to leap from sexless childhood to equally sexless motherhood, as the parent of further cute generations of deodorised Girls Next Door.

Hair colour is important to these female images. To be a regular Girl Next Door, blonde or light brown hair is a must. To be a Tart with a Heart it's best not only to be blonde but dyed. Marilyn Monroe, most famously, personified this creature for the post-war West: sexy, yes, but devoid of threat by being both generous and gullible. Unthreatening, too, because the Tart with a Heart doesn't need to be thought of as a daughter or wife. Monroe may, in her off-screen life, have got through a number of husbands, but it seems, from what we

now know about her death, that Bobby Kennedy was *horrified* at the thought that he, the US attorney general, might have to marry her. As for Monroe's real father, it appears that she never knew him.

The hair of the Scarlet Woman is black or dark red. And, yes, she's usually strong, independent and dangerous to men – which is why she usually comes to a terrible end. Scarlett O'Hara, in the 1939 movie *Gone With the Wind*, may well dig up handfuls of her native earth and cry that she'll never go hungry again, but her independence gives the man she loves, Rhett Butler, all the excuse that he needs to abuse her, physically as well as emotionally.

Gone With the Wind was filmed from the novel of a woman, Margaret Mitchell, which may be why Scarlett doesn't get *totally* crushed: 'Tomorrow,' she swears, as the house lights rise, 'tomorrow is another day.' Other Scarlet Women weren't so lucky. The Egyptian queen, Cleopatra, as portrayed, for instance, by Shakespeare and the movie with Elizabeth Taylor, our old friend the Roman Empress Messalina, Helen of Troy, Bizet's Carmen, Tolstoy's Anna Karenina, all those sultry South American women who lounge around cowboy saloon bars, a hand forever on a hip: all, once exploited for the thrill they give, get hurled under trains, poisoned by asps, stabbed or otherwise discarded.

These images have variations (the Dumb Blonde, the Femme Fatale, the Nymphet, the Nymphomaniac, etc.) but all can restrict women's sexual behaviour by telling them that they've got to decide which 'type' they're going to be belong to: if they're not a virgin and monogamously married, then they must be wildly promiscuous; if they like to study, then they're frigid.

Swingers

The most favoured type of woman in the 1950s – the one considered to be truly feminine, whose image was repeated throughout the pages of the male-owned, male-run fashion magazines – was a kind of cross between the Girl Next Door and the daffy, helpless Dumb Blonde.

Women who'd spent the Second World War assembling aeroplanes, working lathes, running offices and risking their lives as civilians, soldiers and spies, were expected, immediately the war was over, to devote themselves to face creams, bubble baths and petticoats. Women who'd had extramarital affairs while their husbands – no less unfaithful than they were – were training, fighting or prisoners of war, women who'd had 'weekend affairs' with servicemen on forty-eight-hour passes, were abruptly expected to return to chaste or monogamous wholesomeness. And, for approximately 15 years – exhausted by rationing, by sleeplessness, by work both public and domestic – most women did as they were told.

But something happened in 1960 which, if it didn't change things itself, was a sign that the times they were a'changing. As long before as 1928, the British writer D.H. Lawrence had completed a novel called *Lady Chatterley's Lover*. It's very much a hymn of praise to the penis – 'The man looked down the front of his slender white body, and laughed. Between the slim breasts the hair was dark, almost black. But at the root of the belly, where the phallus rose thick and arching, it was gold-red, vivid in a little cloud . . ."Cunt, that's what tha'rt after. Tell lady Jane tha' wants cunt."' – but, if it doesn't show much consideration for women's independent sexuality, it certainly does acknowledge them as lustful beings.

During Lawrence's lifetime, there were pirated editions available in the States and on continental Europe. What happened in 1960 was that the British publishers Penguin brought out an uncut paperback edition, were promptly whipped into court for obscenity and, despite all the judge's advice, were found, by the jury, to be *innocent*. Something was definitely afoot. Perhaps the 'ordinary people' were tired of being told by their olders and richers what their morality should be; perhaps, with full employment and an unprecedented wage growth, they could finally afford to tell the Establishment what to do with its prudery. In any case, all over the West, a sexual revolution had begun.

Unlike in other periods of sexual liberation, the girls were soon able to play with the boys without automatically risking an unwanted pregnancy. In countries free from the Roman Catholic church, in any case, it became, as the 1960s progressed, more and more simple to obtain the Pill – an oral contraceptive available from Family Planning Clinics and doctors and which, if taken punctiliously, is 100 per cent effective.

The concept of the Pill had originated in the head of an American birth control expert, Margaret Sanger, who'd fought for contraceptive education throughout the first part of the century and who, in the early 1960s, had raised $150,000 towards Gregory Pincus's development of a 'simple, cheap, safe contraceptive'. And though we now know that the pill *isn't* safe – in so far as it's been connected with cancer and thrombosis – it certainly allowed those 1960s women to control their reproductiveness themselves – and in such a quick, easy fashion that they seemed to have no more connection with motherhood than men.

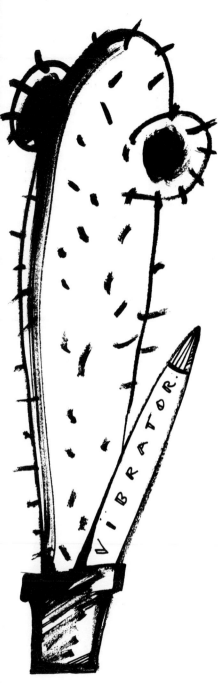

Sex in the 1960s was fun, fun, fun – or else you were doing something wrong. And fun was supposed to be had as often, in as many different ways and with as many different people as was possible. Premarital sex became much more common. In England, in 1964, only 16 per cent of the 15 to 19-year-olds had ever had sex; by 1974, almost half of them had done so. In Sweden, by 1965, 65 per cent of people had had premarital sex. Women also changed partners more often. Forty-three per cent of Danes had had sex with more than one man in 1958; by 1968 the figure was up to 75 per cent. And in the USA in particular (once more, a matter of hygiene?) oral sex was becoming decidedly fashionable. A report in the early 1970s suggested that cunnilingus was practised by half as many kids again as had done so twenty years earlier.

LIBERATION.

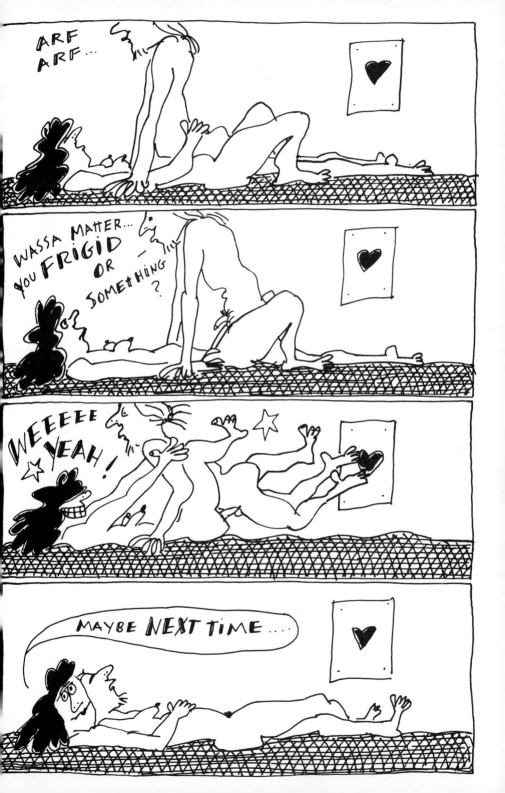

How To Do It books flourished. In *The Sensuous Woman* by 'J' (1969) there were earnest instructions on masturbation ('once you have mastered the vibrator, you should move on to the use of your hands'), kissing, oral and anal sex and what you should wear in bed and what not. (The latter included your glasses, which were 'definitely out'.) Superficially descended from erotic classics like the Indian *Kama Sutra*, or the Chinese *Tao of Love and Sex*, these books, and the magazine articles like them, were, in attitude as much as tone, closer to the instruction manuals that you get when you buy a new blender.

Novels and films in the 1960s were rather less obviously didactic, but the movie of John Braine's *Room at the Top*, which appeared at the beginning of the decade, indicated that sexual frankness was to be the flavour of the day. Its unromantic approach towards the social-climbing screwing of its working-class hero outraged quite a few of its viewers – but was soon eclipsed by a series of startling taboo-breakers.

In 1967, a Swedish film entitled *I am Curious (Yellow)* presented its two central characters fucking in rivers, up trees, on a palace balustrade. In 1968, Andy Warhol's *Lonesome Cowboy* showed heterosexual gang-rape and homosexual fucking. In 1969, there appeared a novel, Philip Roth's *Portnoy's Complaint*, in which male masturbation was the running gag and, symbolically, the central theme. In that same year, the film version of *The Killing of Sister George* by Frank Marcus placed fairly explicit lesbian sex on the family screen for the first time – even if, in doing so, it insisted on making its central characters a 'butch' sadist and a childish, manipulating 'femme'.

Then the 1970 film of Gore Vidal's *Myra Breckinridge* had a scene in which a woman (Mae West) buggered a bumptious young man – while heterosexual buggery the other way round was one component of Bertolucci's movie *Last Tango in Paris* (1973). Some of the above were quite splendid; other were totally awful – but, whether funny, solemn or stupid, each was genuinely trying to explore a range of subjects that had long been confined to the libraries of rich collectors, or pornographic cinema clubs.

With *Last Tango in Paris* we are leaving the 1960s behind – and certainly sexual explicitness didn't just come to an end with the decade. But, for women, the era did have a quite particular sexual flavour, whether they were actually participating in it, felt that they *ought* to be, or loathed it.

In some ways, of course, there was much that was great. Sexual ignorance, hitherto, had been of phenomenal proportions. So, for women in particular, had been the restrictions on their conduct. But, if you look at the archetypal female image of the period – the flat, childish figure (no breasts/stomach gripped by a roll-on), the tights, the short skirts, the pale, baby lips and the large, long-lashed baby eyes – you can see that being 'one of the *boys*' did mean very much what it said. Women might have achieved the 'masculine' right to have a sex life, but they still hadn't got the 'adult' right to decide what its shape might be. As *The Sensuous Woman* makes perfectly clear, women's sexuality turned around men's: 'Naturally you will follow his lead when kissing, but there is a great deal you can do that he can't regard as "taking over". . . .'

And then, of course, 'permissiveness' could become rather like 'compulsion'. Sex could become a desperate competition: a tense, anxiety-inducing act in which a woman would feel continually judged. Instead of asking, 'Am I and are they enjoying this? Yes? Then that's fine. No? Then let's stop,' she was likely to be wondering whether she'd done it enough, with enough different people. Or whether her chest was flushing the way the magazines said that it should. Or whether her nipples were properly erect, or her orgasms suitably multiple. Or, dear god, what was *wrong* with her that she wasn't having orgasms at all?

Besides, all those 'novelties' promoted by the books and the magazines – the all-over kissing, the oral sex, the manual stimulation of genitals – could easily be seen (as indeed they were presented) as trendy trimmings on the 'real thing', as 'foreplay' to make the serious business of sexual intercourse better. A woman who suggested to her male lover that *actually* she got greater pleasure from his kissing and sucking her clitoris or breasts than she did from his penetrant thrusting was likely to be told – and likely to believe – that there had to be something not right with her. Could she, it might be suggested, kindly (since these were liberated times), be a lesbian?

Horror! Shudder! Of course she wasn't. (The image of *The Well of Loneliness* reigned.)

Then perhaps she was frigid?

Even worse – how could a liberated sixties swinger be anything as
awful as frigid? She would have to find the trick of enjoying it – this
thrusting that not just magazines and books, but pop records, films and
TV implied was the apogee of sexual experience. No longer connected
with child-making, sure (unless the woman fucked up), but still the
best thing there could be.

For most of the decade, those two-thirds of women who didn't
enjoy it kept quiet. As did those who'd decided that yes, indeed, their
sexuality *was* lesbian. Freed by access to education and the era's

prosperity from having to marry, they merely developed an alternative culture, ignoring men to whatever extent their working lives permitted.

Even among those fabled, long-haired, peace-loving, gentle hippies, the women were often living on men's terms alone, whether stirring rice in the kitchen of the commune, or lying back on the Indian bedspread for yet another Great Fuck.

Although Betty Friedan's *The Feminine Mystique*, questioning the post-war role of women, was first published in 1963, it wasn't until the end of the decade that women, generally, started expressing and formulating their doubts.

Sisters

Feminism since the late 1960s hasn't, of course, been entirely concerned with women's *sexual* experience. Constitutional politics, employment, child care, education, the arts, the sciences, language, war, religion: anything you care to name has been swept into the post-1960s feminist debate.

But – perhaps because of the era from which this feminist movement emerged – a woman's right to sexual pleasure, fulfilment and freedom of choice has been pivotal to it in a way that it wasn't for earlier feminist movements. Many of the pace-setting 1970s texts – Germaine Greer's *The Female Eunuch* (1970), Kate Millett's *Sexual Politics* (1970), Sulamith Firestone's *The Dialectic of Sex* (1971) – put sex quite firmly at the centre of the stage, presenting it not just as incidental, as a luxury to be dealt with when crèches and equal pay had been sorted out, but as a facet of women's experience that reflected on all the others. Similarly, feminists in France have used the sexual analyses of philosopher Michel Foucault and, more directly, psychiatrist Jacques Lacan as the starting point for many of their most urgent and productive writings.

A woman's 'right to her body' might well have seemed a peculiar idea to eighteenth-century or Victorian women, with their limited access to contraception, abortion, bottle-feeding, lovers, money. To present-day women, on the other hand, it's both desirable and feasible.

And the use of women's bodies as *objects* has, in a whole variety of ways, been one of the sexual traditions that present-day women have questioned and attacked. Rape – described by the feminist writer and speaker Andrea Dworkin as 'the dirtiest four-letter word in the English language' – has been exposed for the all-too-common, day-to-day event that it is. Almost everyone is appalled when sexual intercourse is forced on children, virgins or very old women – or when a rapist severely injures, mutilates or murders his victim(s) – but women have recently shed their light on the less sensational, far more common instances of rape in our society: rapes where the victim has decided not to struggle, thus avoiding being beaten or stabbed, rapes where the threat has been financial, emotional or social, rapes by acquaintances, lovers, husbands, rapes of prostitutes by clients or others. All of these happen every day – yet most go unreported because the victims believe that the police will be unsympathetic. (In a 1985 London survey, *Ask Any Woman* by Ruth E. Hall, 17 per cent of the 1,236 respondents admitted that they'd been raped – and, of these, only *8 per cent* had been to the police with what had happened.)

The American feminist Susan Brownmiller has analysed rape, in *Against Our Will*, as 'a conscious process of intimidation by which *all men* keep *all women* in a state of fear' – and many women now perceive it as an act which merely epitomises heterosexual sex: as a caricature, in other words, of men's 'taking' and 'having' of women in ordinary intercourse.

Others urge strongly against this analysis. 'I find it absurd,' wrote Simone de Beauvoir, 'to assume that all coitus is rape. By saying that, one agrees to the masculine myth that a man's sex is a sword, a weapon. The real problem is to find new sexual relations which will not be oppressive.'

Black women in white-ruled societies – where rape scares and accusations have been used as a means of repressing black men – tend to keep a distance from this white debate. But, as black activist Angela Davis wrote in 1981: 'That Black women have not joined the anti-rape movement en masse does not, therefore, mean that they oppose anti-rape measures in general.'

As central as the anti-rape movement has been contemporary feminists' drive against pornography. Indeed, by some, the two have been seen as directly connected abuses, since, by both, women are reduced to passive objects of desire – to nothing more than the inanimate shoe, or pair of lacy French knickers, that a fetishist might use to achieve his sexual satisfaction. 'Pornography is the theory,' goes one feminist slogan, 'rape is the practice.'

One of the problems with opposing pornography, however, is that of being clear where pornography ends and erotica begins. Both, after all, are concerned with sex – my dictionary defines erotic: 'of, concerning, or arousing sexual desire or giving sexual pleasure'; pornographic: 'Of writings, pictures, films, etc., designed to stimulate sexual excitement' – and *erotic* art, I should like to suggest, was one of humanity's better ideas. The film *Last Tango in Paris*, with its intense, exclusive concentration on two people's mutual lust, the wonderfully funny sexiness of Noel Coward's play *Private Lives*, Colette's novel *Claudine a l'école*, Auguste Rodin's sculpture *The Kiss*: those, among others, are erotic works that I should be sorry never to have seen.

Anyone else, however, could find the list either puzzling or disgusting – which implies that the feminist Ellen Willis might well have had a good point when she wrote, in 1981, 'In practice, attempts to sort out good erotica from bad porn inevitably come down to What turns me on is erotica; what turns you on is pornographic.'

But other feminists have persevered – pinpointing, in particular, the way pornographic images of women (as distinct from erotic images) appeal to men's violence and desire for dominance, the way in which they represent women as 'dehumanized sexual objects' (Andrea Dworkin). Images of women beaten, bound, gagged, helpless, not enjoying themselves: all of these reinforce the notion that women's bodies are for men to *use*, that their own sexuality is irrelevant. And whether they appear in acknowledged pornography or, more insidiously, in advertising, women have certainly become more aware of how such images threaten them.

Still, still, it's not simple. Very few feminist women could support the restrictive legislation, now afoot in the West, whereby any representation of sex which isn't of straightforward, heterosexual intercourse is in danger of being forbidden. As American poet Adrienne Rich made clear in *Compulsory Heterosexuality and Lesbian Existence* (1980), there are already far too many attempts to limit the range and diversity of women's sexual expression.

And then a novel called *The Story of O*, which centres pretty exclusively round its female protagonist's masochism, has been read and found to be erotic by any number of women. As Lynne Segal wrote in 1983:

I suspect that some of the emotional horror feminists and other women feel towards sexist pornography (which I share) is not simply that they think it encourages men to rape and objectify women (there is no evidence that they need pornography for that), but that it is obnoxious because it both degrades and titillates us. And that is *not* a connection which we like ... it is not unusual for feelings we dislike to seem to come from somewhere else, when in fact they are buried inside us as well as reflected in the social world which shaped them to begin with.

The recent debate in much of the West on the subject of women's sado-masochism has also been trying to take on board those feelings that are 'buried inside us'. Sado-masochistic sex (S&M) is essentially concerned with dominance and submission: with lovers becoming aroused and gratified either by humiliating (sometimes hurting) their partner, or, alternatively, being hurt and/or humiliated themselves. Even though the word 'sadistic' is derived from the eighteenth/nineteenth-century Marquis de Sade, and the word 'masochistic' from the nineteenth-century Leopold von Masoch, it's highly unlikely that lovers before them never got pleasure from such role-playing. More to the point, though, many women perceive male dominance and female submission as precisely what heterosexual relations have always, disastrously involved – not only in bed, but around the house, in public, legally, financially – and, because of this, regarded S&M with quite understandable distaste. In increasing numbers, since the late 1960s, they have been trying to formulate relations (both heterosexual and lesbian) where neither partner abuses the other with power.

Which was why there was such an outcry, in 1982, on the publication by an American lesbian/feminist organisation of *Coming to Power*, a collection of writings which advocated S&M.

Its proponents have stressed that S&M is the enactment of 'fantasy', and have argued that dominance/submission desires are better expressed than repressed, but other feminists have not been terribly amused. S&M, wrote Kathleen Barry, in the year that *Coming to Power* was published, is 'a leftist insurgency against feminism and the newest threat to feminist anti-rape and anti-pornography activism'.

In 1985, the London Lesbian and Gay Centre was torn by a motion to exclude overt practitioners of S&M. But whatever views a woman might have, on this or on any other subject affecting her sex life, one achievement of present-day feminists has been to construct the critical frameworks, the platforms, the general self-confidence, from which all women may continue to explore, develop and define their sexuality.

And that doesn't mean – as is sometimes maintained – a tiny handful of academic or politically activist women. *The Woman Book of Love and Sex* (1985), a survey of 15,000 readers of *Woman* magazine in Britain, indicates a growing assumption on the part of women of all sorts and ages that *their* sexuality matters – and a growing awareness of the cultural pressures that hinder or prevents its fulfilment.

'I always have an orgasm either before or after intercourse, but sometimes I feel pressured by the press and films and books because I have never had an orgasm during intercourse. I need manual stimulation. . . .'

'How can you tell a man that, far from being every woman's fantasy, [his penis] being bigger than normal is a problem. My husband is well endowed and sex is so uncomfortable I try to avoid it. My lover was if anything smaller than average and I could enjoy the whole act. . . .'

'My friend got such a thrill bringing me to a climax that she kept doing it time and time again. Naturally, I did not want her to stop. I felt a beautiful warm feeling when we kissed and cuddled. It was much more real than can ever be possible with any man. . . .'

'I thought of sex as being something for the men. I worried if they thought I was doing it right. Through masturbating I learned what I like. . . .'

SOMETHING

The book, of course, has its stories of guilt, confusion and resignation, but perhaps the most important thing that this feminist movement has achieved is, from its very earliest days, to promote an atmosphere where women didn't see one another as rivals (for men) but as people with whom one's sexual worries and fears could be shared – and exorcised. This process, in turn, led to women involved in heterosexual relationships acquiring the confidence to correct their partners' media-reinforced assumptions.

'Do you think you might be a lesbian?' could now, more easily, be answered: 'No, I don't, not necessarily. Quite a few of the women I've talked to don't find sexual intercourse satisfying. . . .'

'Well, all the women *I've* ever fucked . . .'

'. . . and an awful lot of them fake it, just to keep the men happy.'

And – since men aren't *all* perverse, obdurate or simply stupid, progress was under way. Or else the dialogue might go like this:

'Do you think you might be a lesbian?'

'Yes, as it happens, I probably am. I'm terribly fond of you John, but this must be goodbye.'

In learning to value one another as sisters, as friends, as political and personal support, 'heterosexual' women in the 1970s and 1980s rediscovered each other's potential as lovers. While from the other direction, so to speak, those 'lesbian' women who had kept themselves within a specifically homosexual culture (whether politically active or not) began to emerge from their gay brothers' shadow, dispelling the Butch/Femme, Bitter-and-Babycham image of popular fears and providing their sisters with alternatives to traditional, heterosexual structures: strong support groups of friends, non-possessive relationships, communal living, sex between equals, confidence as women alone.

Coming through

A history of sex can no more *finish* than a history of politics or agriculture. Unless or until the world is destroyed, there'll continue to be new inventions, discoveries, outside events and internal ideas to shape how we see ourselves sexually: how we behave, think and feel when we fuck.

As I write, there seems to be much to be hoped for. In far greater numbers than at any time before, especially if they live in the big cities, women in the twentieth-century West have the possibility of living their sex lives as they want to: of exploring their sexuality free from history's most iniquitous social and physical constraints; of understanding the ins and outs of their complex, erotic desires; of expressing themselves; of asking questions; of coming up with some answers.

But the force of the 'sexual backlash' – the growing clamour that women hand back those sexual freedoms that they've only now begun to accumulate – cannot be blithely ignored. Large sections of the media, for instance, have presented the current epidemic of genital herpes – a virus quite often, though not inevitably, spread through sexual contact, and which causes periodic eruptons of painful blisters on the genitals – as a punishment, a Plague of Boils, that Bad Women have brought on themselves.

The newer AIDS, which destroys the sufferer's immunity to fatal illnesses, has been presented in a similar light. Originally seen as a curse on homosexual men who go in for anal sex (since blood is the means by which it's most often transmitted), it encouraged not only the media, but politicians, doctors, the police and morticians, to indulge in attacks on gay men *and* lesbian women (though the latter, in fact, are the sexually active group least likely to get it). In other words, instead of being seen as the terrible tragedy it is, instead of urgent attempts being made to discover methods for curing it, instead of information pouring out on how it can best be prevented – the major institutional response was at first a murderous apathy, coupled with an insinuation that sexual 'deviants' deserve what they get. Now, however, governments are seeing that the AIDS virus is a threat to heterosexual people as well (even to those who never have sex, since it's carried by blood as well as by semen) and they've started to make a few scrambling

gestures to prevent or minimise its spread. But, simultaneously, the feeling is growing that *all* sex may be 'evil' – except for the monogamous and preferably married variety.

Which is patently illogical. The sensible part of the anti-AIDS programme has nothing to do with 'evil' or 'good', or even with limiting sexual arousal, pleasure and satisfaction. It's the part initially promoted by the gay community: the information on 'safe' sex. This includes wearing condoms for anal and vaginal penetration – but it also reminds us of other, non-penetrant routes towards sexual satisfaction.

And, in any case, it really is time that penetrant sex was dethroned. Sexual intercourse, especially, needs shaking down from its pedestal. Sex for humans has never, as we've seen, been a simple baby-making mechanism: it's been about sensual pleasure as well, about giving and receiving love, about fun. And sexual intercourse isn't the only, or even the best thing for any of these.

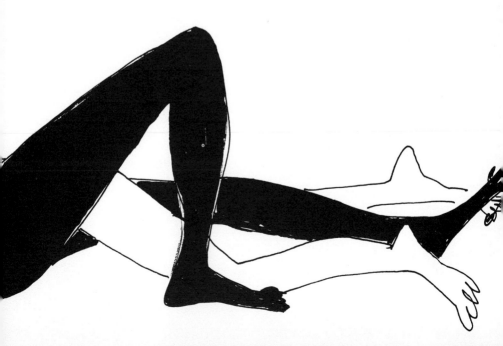

Of course, some people, women included, may like it better than anything on earth – but ever since women have actually been *asked* it's transpired that most of them don't. A report from the 1930s, *A Thousand Marriages* by Dickinson and Bream, concluded that sexual intercourse was unsatisfactory for two in three of the 1,000 women they'd interviewed. And Masters and Johnson, in the 1960s, observed of those women they'd studied in laboratories: 'The lowest intensity of target-organ response was achieved during coition.' And Seymour Fisher's 1970s study, *The Female Orgasm*, estimated that only 39 per cent of women came through intercourse. And *The Hite Report* put it as low as 30 per cent. And *The Woman Book of Love and Sex* reports on women's orgasms: 'only 42 per cent of wives and 24 per cent of unmarried women who reach orgasm usually do so through inter-course.' Over half a century, the figures have been pretty consistent.

And none of it is surprising. Not only is the vagina itself almost entirely nerveless, but the clitoris (*alive* with nerves) is not guaranteed to be stimulated by straightforward penetrant sex. As early as the 1940s, sexologist Dr Helena Wright had debunked the idea that 'women will have an answering orgasm felt in the vagina induced by the movement of the penis' and expressed grave doubts about 'the efficacy of the penis-vagina combination for producing orgasm for a woman'. But as Anne Koedt wrote in *The Myth of the Vaginal Orgasm* (1970):

> One of the elements of male chauvinism is the refusal or inability to see women as total, separate human beings . . . men have chosen to define women only in terms of how they benefit men's lives. Sexually, a woman is not seen as an individual wanting to share equally in the sexual act, any more than she was seen as a person with independent desires when she did anything else in society. Thus, it is easy for men to make up what facts are convenient about women, as society is controlled so that women have not been organized to form even a vocal opposition to male 'experts'.

If, as has been frequently claimed, 'a cock and a cunt are made for each other', it really is only true in so far as creating new human beings is concerned. For sexual pleasure and fulfilment, the conjunction of clitoris with lips, tongues, hands – or, indeed, of penis with the same –

is more suitable. And not just for women, but for men as well, since one of sexual intercourse's many drawbacks is that, while it's happening, neither party can focus too well on the pleasure they're *giving* – and sex (however paradoxically) is one of the few activities where even the least altruistic among us gets genuine, unforced, unpremeditated pleasure from giving pleasure to another.

In demolishing the myth of intercourse as the *pinnacle* of sexual experience, it would, of course, be lunacy itself to insist on some specific alternative. Understanding our own desires, both what they are and why they are; talking (and listening) to one another; believing in ourselves (instead of believing the distorting mirrors that get flashed in our face); loving ourselves enough to require that those whom we love love us back; continuing to alter the social structures that cramp, hurt or do damage to us; continuing to assert our existence: our needs, our angers, our delights – it's things such as these that will determine whether the girls and women who follow us shrivel from the very mention of sex, or embrace it with mouths, breasts and thighs.

Books to beg, borrow or buy

Balmer, Josephine (trans. and intro.) (1984), *Sappho: Poems and Fragments*, London, Brilliance Books.

Balsdon, J.P.V.D. (1983), *Roman Women: Their History and Habits*, New York, Barnes & Noble (first published 1962).

Barnstone, A. and Barnstone, W. (1980), *A Book of Women Poets from Antiquity to Now*, New York, Schocken Books.

Coote, Anna and Campbell, Beatrix (1982), *Sweet Freedom*, Oxford, Blackwell.

Figes, Eva (1978), *Patriarchal Attitudes*, London, Virago (first published 1970).

Gathorne-Hardy, Jonathan (1981), *Love, Sex, Marriage and Divorce*, London, Cape.

Janssen-Jurreit, Marielouise (1982), *Sexism*, London, Pluto (first published 1976).

Klaich, Dolores (1974), *Woman Plus Woman*, New York, Simon & Schuster.

Kramarae, Cheris and Treichler, Paula A. (1985), *A Feminist Dictionary*, London, Pandora Press.

Lewis, Jane (1984), *Women in England 1870-1950*, Brighton, Wheatsheaf.

Mead, Margaret (1977), *Sex and Temperament in Three Primitive Societies*, London, Routledge & Kegan Paul (first published 1936).

Monaghan, Patricia (1981), *Women in Myth and Legend*, London, Junction Books.

Parrinder, Edward Geoffrey (1980), *Sex in the World's Religions*, London, Sheldon Press.

Rowbotham, Sheila (1977), *Hidden from History*, London, Pluto Press.

Sanders, Deirdre (1985), *The Woman Book of Love and Sex*, London, Sphere.

Shaw, Evelyn and Darling, Joan (1985), *Strategies of Being Female: Animal Patterns, Human Choices*, Brighton, Harvester.

Shostak, Marjorie (1982), *Nisa: Life and Words of a !Kung Woman*, London, Allen Lane.
Spender, Dale (1983), *Women of Ideas*, London, Routledge & Kegan Paul.
Wells, Jess (1982), *A Herstory of Prostitution in Western Europe*, Berkeley, Shameless Hussy.

SEX SEX SEX SEX SEX SEX

DEFINITELY
AN
ACQUIRED
TASTE.